SOWING TEACHABLE MOMENTS YEAR ONE

24 Memorable Lessons

Kent McClain

destinēe

SOWING TEACHABLE MOMENTS YEAR ONE
24 Memorable Lessons

By Kent McClain

Copyright © 2012 Kent McClain
ISBN: 978-1-938367-03-8
Publication date: January 2013
Published by Destinée Media: www.destineemedia.com
Cover design: Scott Davis www.scottdaviscreative.com
Interior design: Per-Ole Lind www.perolelind.com
Interior layout: Ralph McCall
Set with Bembo and Akzidenz-Grotesk BQ

Scripture taken from the New American Standard Bible
Copyright 1960, 1962, 1963, 1968, 1971, 1972, 1973,
1975, 1987, 1988. The Lockman Foundation. Used
by permission

Dedicated to
Brodie and Shannon

My two children who filled my life with love,
joy, and countless Teachable Moments

WITH GRATITUDE

I want to thank all of those who took my manuscript and fine-tuned it with their editing skills, biblical insight, and wise suggestions. These special people include: Kelli Brown (school staff editor and grammatical genius), Ralph McCall (author, parent, and loyal friend), Wendell Wellman (Hollywood screen writer, consultant, and longtime friend), Myrna McClain (school teacher, devoted parent and grandparent), Shannon Allen (realtor, dedicated wife, and short-term missionary), and Brodie McClain (pastor, missionary, and loving parent)

Finally, a great deal of appreciation and gratitude goes to my entire family and many friends, who encouraged me through prayer and support while writing Sowing Teachable Moments Year One.

CONTENTS

Teachable Moments

Introduction   1

The **S** in **TIPS** for Parenting   7
(Sowing the Word by means of a Teachable Moment)

Special holidays

1. Trick or Treat *(Halloween)*   9

2. The Thanksgiving President *(Thanksgiving)*   14

3. Colors and Symbols of Christmas *(Christmas)*   19

4. The Star of Bethlehem *(Christmas)*   23

5. Resolutions *(New Year's Eve)*   26

6. Lincoln the Christian *(President's Day)*   29

7. All is Lost; All is Restored! *(Easter)*   33

8. Silent Saturday *(Easter)*   38

9. The End is Even Better *(Mother's Day)*   42

10. Plan B *(Father's Day)*   46

Important beliefs and practices of the Christian life

11. Journaling   50
(Helping your children remember what God has done)

12. Filling the Bucket *(Acts of kindness)*   55

13.	Tares on the Freeway *(Why God allows evil)*	58
14.	Holly Love *(God's unconditional love)*	64
15.	Narnia *(Virtuous literature/movies can help build your children's faith)*	67
16.	Laura Crow *(Assurances in the Christian life)*	73
17.	"No," "Not Yet," "Yes" *(Teaching children what to expect)*	79
18.	12 Cans *(Faith)*	85
19.	Be Like Joseph *(Persevering through anger)*	93
20.	Tears Are Okay *(Teaching children how to comfort the grieving)*	97
21.	The Man on the High-Flying Trapeze *(Faith leading to salvation)*	100
22.	The Ghost and the Darkness *(The influences of the flesh and Satan)*	105
23.	God the Father, Son, and Spirit *(Explaining the Trinity)*	111
24.	A Break in the Dam *(The Spirit's entrance after salvation)*	119

Conclusion	124
Reference Notes	125
Destinee Media	128

INTRODUCTION

Teachable Moment illustrations of Christ's tomb
*(These were constructed by my sixth grade class of 1993
to serve as a remembrance of Easter)*

Those twelve stones which they had taken from the Jordan, Joshua set up at Gilgal. He said to the sons of Israel, when your children ask their fathers in time to come, saying, "What are these stones?" Then you shall inform your children, saying, "Israel crossed this Jordan on dry ground." For the Lord your God dried up the waters of the Jordan before you until you had crossed, just as the Lord your God had done to the Red Sea, which He dried up before us until we had crossed; that all the peoples of the earth may know that the hand of the Lord is mighty, so that you may fear the Lord your God forever.
(Joshua 4:20-24)

Sowing Teachable Moments Year One is the companion text to the book, *Teachable Moments (Teaching Children How to Remember God's Truth)*. It comprises 24 biblically-based lessons you can use with your children over a year. *Sowing Teachable Moments* is the last part of the TIPS acronym introduced in *Teachable Moments,* the book. In review, TIPS represents the four essential parts in discipling your children. The **T** represents the importance of **teaching** your children the Word; the **I** stands for the great value in building **intimate** relationships with them; **P** denotes **preparing** your kids for the world and future ahead, and the **S** stands for **sowing** illustrative and memorable lessons into the hearts of your children so they never forget.

Only 24 lessons are listed as this is all most families will have time to handle during the course of a year and that is okay. In fact, it is better to take your time doing each lesson than to rush through to get them all done.

On the other hand, you may find that after doing a few, you will want to do more. If so, then go to my web site (www.tmoments.com) there are several more there to download and explore.

The format for each Teachable Moment lesson in this book is simple. It includes the title with its description, an overall representative Scripture, the teaching itself, a Teachable Moment exercise, and several supportive Scriptures in parenthesis. The Scriptures in parenthesis are two-fold in purpose: to establish a biblical foundation for what has been taught, and to add depth to your lesson.

To look up and read each verse is very important, because this builds a reservoir of Scriptural knowledge for both you and your children. The Spirit can then take that knowledge, if you let Him, and use it to help each one of you deal with the many false teachings and values of this world. The Spirit will also use your growing knowledge of the Word to help you make important decisions down the road, whether as a parent or child. (John 14:26; John 16:13)

Before I introduce the 24 Teachable Moments and give some final thoughts on how to carry them out, let me share with you a related experience with my own kids while hiking to Half Dome in Yosemite National Park. The hike took all day because it was 16 miles round trip, an 8000 foot ascent, and included a six-story-long cable at the end to reach the top.

The hike took place in the summer and we began about 7:30 in the morning. We started early as we didn't want to get caught making our way back at night. My son and daughter had been on this hike and parts of it when they were younger. I particularly remember on one occasion, carrying my daughter on my shoulders when she was about six years old. This time around both Brodie and Shannon were in their twenties and married. As we began our ascent, there was the mist trail to climb first, which was the toughest part of the hike. It was difficult because it went straight up, and climbers were continuously pelted with a heavy rainy mist from Vernal Falls.

After getting past the falls, we all rested, including Nic, my daughter's husband who came with us. Although we were glad to be done with the mist trail, there were still six or seven more miles to reach the top. As we walked, I began sharing my first experience climbing to Half Dome. I was about 21 years old on a church youth trip. During that Yosemite outing, the youth director Sonny, asked if anyone would like to try to hike to Half

Dome with him. Several of us guys said, "Sure, why not, it can't be that hard." So, we all started off from the bottom, but as we hit the half-way point at Nevada Falls, most bailed out and went back, including Sonny. Three of us, Don, Jim, and I, decided to keep going and finally made it to the top that afternoon.

While sharing this story with Brodie, Shannon, and Nic, I also told them of the great spiritual experiences I had during that trip, as well as so many others to Yosemite that followed. I went on and told them I felt that God used this beautiful place to remind me over and over again of the many truths I had learned through the years, especially in regard to His grace and majesty. They are what I would call now Teachable Moments.

As we walked further up the trail, getting ready to traverse back and forth across some tough cut-backs, we all decided to make up some new Teachable Moments to pass the time. Brodie started things off by saying that the Christian life was like the rainy mist trail at times, difficult to see where you were going. This was because of the pelting rain of temptation and false teachings the world throws at you. Then he added that if you just hang in there, trusting God one step of faith at a time, you will get through it to the top, so to speak.

Shannon chimed in and said, "The mist trail is often like what we do when tough times come; we put our heads down to protect our eyes and wonder if we'll ever get through to the top. But if we would just stop and look up for a second, we'd be encouraged to see that the end was closer than we thought, and well worth the hike."

Nic pointed out that after getting to the top, we would be able to look out from a new vantage point and see all of Yosemite and its great beauty, just as we will be able to see God's overall beautiful plan in our lives. I said, "A hike like this is so much better when traveling together, for if one falters or gets discouraged, the rest are there to help, and so it is in the Christian life when fellowshipping and teaming up with other believers along the way.

When nearing the top, God gave me another Teachable Moment I will never forget. It wasn't anything like the mist trail, or the view from the top, but rather it was a person we met that day on the trail. As my daughter was helping me take those last steps to the Dome, I looked up and, low and behold, there was Sonny hiking down from it. I couldn't believe my eyes! Here was my youth pastor, who had challenged me to climb Half Dome with him 36 years ago almost to the day. While we talked and shared experiences, a flood of memories came to me. Not only did I have memories of experiences on that first trip but of other trips as well, particularly when I brought my own youth groups to Yosemite.

Finally, in looking back at this Half Dome hike, the most noteworthy part of it was not so much the beauty we saw or even being together on the hike, but the great truths we learned together by associating God's Word with what we were experiencing. This is what Teachable Moments is all about, linking God's many truths with what is seen or experienced. Just as my kids were able to come up with their own Teachable Moments, even after they had grown up, so will yours if you start with them right away.

What's Ahead

The following 24 Teachable Moment articles are split into two sections: the first 10 focus on teachings linked to different holidays, and the final 14 explore some of the most important beliefs and practices of the Christian life. The Scriptures used throughout this book were primarily from the New American Standard Version of the Bible. The final count ended up to be 1138 verses in 364 passages.

The Biblical Examples

Like the three sections (teaching, intimacy, and preparation) in my *Teachable Moments* book, God the Father, Son, and Spirit will be used as the models to follow, with a little more emphasis on the Spirit. Unlike the book, where only one or two biblical characters were referenced to gain a human example, many will be included in these articles. George Washington, Abraham Lincoln, Lillian Trasher, Jacob Deshazer, are just some examples. In respect to quoting Scripture, I once again used either "..." or **"rbk"** (revised by Kent) when leaving out non-essential words or verses for the sake of brevity.

Final thoughts

There are a few final suggestions to consider when carrying out a Teachable Moment. First, if your children are very young, you may only be able to do the Teachable Moment exercise with them at the end. If so, then read the article to yourself to get the main thrust of what's taught. Then carry out the exercise with your children, explaining as much as you can.

If they are old enough to listen to a full reading of the Teachable Moment, be sure to take your time. Most children, with few exceptions, absorb much more when they are not rushed. Therefore, plan a time when you can address their questions, thoughts, and opinions while doing the Teachable Moment. If both of your schedules are pressed, then think outside of the box before rushing to complete the Teachable Moment. For example, our family did a devotional version of Teachable Moments in our car for seven years, as we traveled back and forth to school and work.

We lived in Los Angeles where most families spend a lot of their time on the freeways. Instead of being frustrated, we took advantage of this time; we recited the Scriptures, read a few Christian books, did some Teachable Moments, and prayed for one another and others. All in all, we spent about 500 hours doing this, which was important because both of our kids went through adolescence during this time. Kids going through this part of their lives can be a challenge, but not as much when there is a constant dose of God's truth and good communication going on between you and them.

When you are doing a Teachable Moment, it is important not to lecture too much to your children. They get plenty of lectures at school and even at church; they don't need another during their Teachable Moment time with you. In order to curb lecturing, let your children read the teaching portion if they are old enough. Encourage them to state what they believe is being taught. Allow them to freely express what they are learning, no matter what that ends up being. If they are as engaged as you in the Teachable Moment, they will love it. If you just lecture them, they may mentally turn off after awhile.

It is also important when doing a Teachable Moment to display a real spirit of humility in your children's presence. To accomplish this, be transparent with them during your study time together by openly admitting the areas of the lesson you need work on. A mother or father who is truly humble will not hesitate to tell their children that they have not arrived yet; that just like them, they too are a work in progress with God.

If necessary, do a Teachable Moment in two or three sessions. The Teachable Moment #23 on the Trinity is one that may require this.

Finally, don't hesitate to repeat doing a Teachable Moment a second or third time with your children, especially one your whole family enjoyed. You might even want to add new parts to its illustration or new biblical insights the second and third time around. Repetition is good; Jesus, Himself, repeated several messages over and over again with the disciples. During His first year, He taught them about His role on earth at least a dozen times.[1] If Jesus used repetition with the disciples, you should follow His example with your children.

As they grow older, you may find your children wanting to lead the Teachable Moment time because they are very familiar with the lesson and feel confident to do so. If you can get them to this point, you have done a great job of discipling, because now they are not just listeners of the Word; they are teachers of it. And that's real good!

The S in TIPS for Parenting
(Sowing the Word by means of a Teachable Moment)

And He was teaching them many things in parables, and was saying to them in His teaching, "Listen to this! ..."
(Mark 4:2-3)

This section is based on 1131 verses in 361 passages of Scripture

---

Thoughts ahead

The answer to the question of why God still allows evil and those who practice it to exist, has to do with the choice God gives to everyone born into this world to either believe or reject Him. (From the article, Tares on the Freeway)

God always answers every prayer and does so immediately. This is a truth your children need to learn while they are young, because you don't want them believing that God didn't answer their prayers when actually He did. (From the article, "No," "Not Yet," "Yes")

The most important point concerning the ministry of the Spirit is that whatever decisions you or your children make, the Spirit will never leave you. (From the article, Break in the Dam)

TEACHABLE MOMENT 1
TRICK OR TREAT
(Halloween)

…but I want you to be wise in what is good and innocent in what is evil.
(Romans 16:19)

The following article was taken out of *The Bakersfield Californian*, our local Bakersfield, California newspaper, a number of years ago. It was actually authored by Laura Stepp from the Washington Post who gave me permission to use her article.[1] There are two terms (pimp and ho) in this article with which you may not be acquainted. The term pimp refers to a man who makes his living managing prostitutes. Ho is the current term for a prostitute.

According to your children's age and understanding, you may want to skip this first part concerning the pimps and hos. If so, then move to the history of Halloween and the Teachable Moment that follows.

"Hey Mom! Hey Dad! We've found the perfect Halloween costumes for kids." What Josh and Caitlin need are the rags that are selling briskly in California and New York: Child pimp suits and "ho" dresses. At $40 to $50, they begin at size 4, tailored in the '70's style of blaxploitation movies like "Superfly." Can't you see little Josh in a pink velvet suit and matching wide-brimmed hat with faux-zebra trim? Or Caitlin in black feathers and stockings as she sets off to trick or treat for UNICEF?" (The outfit actually looks like a 1920's flapper dress, but don't tell her that. It would spoil her pose. And right now, it's sold out because of "overwhelming demand," says one Web site).

You think we're kidding. We're not. Brandsonsale.com, an online marketing company that sells everything from poker chips to bandanas, is offering one ho and four pimp costumes for children this year for Halloween, along with its usual Spiderman, Oatmeal Bear, witches, devils, and vampires.

Next year, the company plans pimp attire for infants. The demand, says company spokesman Jonathon Weeks Jr., grows each year. "We started with the pimp suit two years ago," Weeks said from his Cerritos office. "It's one of our biggest sellers. We also sell pimp and ho outfits to whole families: Mom, Dad, kids, and the dog." His customers span the racial and ethnic rainbow, he says. Most live in California, New York and Florida: "You know where the real pimps hang out."

Teen-agers out of earshot of adults, call one another "pimp" and "ho" the way past generations used "dude" and "girlfriend." One customer of Brandsonsale is Abigail Potter, of Greer, S.C. Last Halloween, her sons Justin and Aaron spotted a school friend wearing a pimp costume. This year, the boys, 10 and 11 talked Potter into ordering two-- one pink, one purple—for a neighborhood Halloween party. "I know some people will make a big deal about it," Potter says, "but come on, it's Halloween. Let's not take things too seriously. One son makes straight A's, the other A's and B's. They're good children who wanna get a laugh."

It is amazing that Halloween is now moving toward adoration of pimps and hos, but anything with an evil root always degenerates and worsens as time passes. Halloween is one of our celebrated holidays with a definite evil root and origin. In the 1950's Halloween appeared harmless, but as each decade passes the holiday has worsened with poisoned candy, gang violence, and destruction of property. Whereas kids were once allowed to roam their local neighborhoods with friends, now they must be escorted by caring adults for their own safety, and when the kids get home, the candy must be carefully checked.

The costumes have traditionally been demonic for the most part. Without realizing it, parents put their children in costumes (witches, warlocks, monsters, skeletons, and ghosts) rooted in devil worship, misery, fear, and death. They say it is all in fun, but it is more than fun for Satan worshipers; it is a day in which they revel because of the honor bestowed on them by what is worn in their name. Now, Halloween is sinking to a new low by dressing up innocent children in pimp and ho (whore) costumes.

The History of Halloween

If you are unclear about the root of evil in Halloween, here is a short history. The origin of Halloween is the Celtic festival of Samhain. The Celtics lived in what is now Great Britain, Ireland, and northern France. Their new year began on November 1st, and the festival that began the previous evening honored Samhain, the Celtic lord of death. It marked the beginning of winter, a time of coldness and death. They built a bonfire and burned animals, crops, and even human sacrifices to honor their god of death.

During the 1800s, large numbers of immigrants from this area of the world brought this evil practice to America and renamed it Halloween. The practice of trick or treating (a Celtic custom) became the most noted custom of our new Halloween celebration. It was meant to be a harmless time where children dressed up as witches, goblins, and other frightening and evil creatures, to supposedly, in fun, scare neighbors into giving them candy.

Yet, have you ever wondered how trick or treating ever came about with the Celts? Part of this Celtic ritual was a belief that dead souls would return to their original homes. The people were terrified of these evil spirits and they would place sweet goodies on their doorsteps to appease them. Their belief was if the evil spirits liked their treat they would leave them alone, but if they didn't, they would trick them by casting evil spells on them similar to the ones cast in the Harry Potter films. Sad to say, our trick or treating evolved from this tradition.

Halloween was not party time for the Celtic people. They feared the evil spirits roaming the earth on October 31st, so they stayed home. If someone was forced to leave the house, he would disguise himself as a demon to fool the evil spirits.

Other Halloween traditions, such as the fear of a black cat, are also not without a root of evil. The Celtics believed that humans were punished for their evil deeds by changing them into black cats. Therefore, it was quite proper to sacrifice a black cat in a ritualistic bonfire on October 31st.

Even something that seems as innocent as a Jack-o-lantern had a dark beginning. This tradition comes from a legend about a man named Jack who was turned away from heaven because of his wickedness. He was also turned away from hell because he had played tricks on the devil. Therefore, he was sentenced to spend the rest of his days roaming the earth as a demonic spirit, haunting anyone who crossed his path. The legend says he carved a face in a turnip and put a candle in it to guide him at night to his next victim. We have now substituted a pumpkin for a Jack-o-lantern at Halloween.[2]

Most holidays celebrated in America are rooted in something good or significant: Christmas is the birth of a Savior, Lincoln's birthday is the celebration of a great President who liberated the slaves in our country, and Memorial Day honors those who made America free through their sacrifice on the battlefield. Not so for Halloween. It is a celebration of evil, and we should never take any delight of evil lightly, no matter how innocent it seems. *(Ephesians 6:10-17; Deuteronomy 18:9-14)*

Teachable Moment

What should Christians do with the Halloween holiday? There are three plausible biblical alternatives.

1. In evidence of your stand against evil of any kind, you are certainly within the bounds of Scripture to reject this holiday completely and condemn any participation in it. If you take this approach, then your kids should not dress up in any costume and should forgo trick or treating. An evening dedicated to praying for the lost might be a better use of your time.

"Therefore, come out from their midst and be separate," says the Lord. "And do not touch what is unclean." (II Corinthians. 6:17)

2. A second alternative is to make a ministry out of the evening by witnessing to those in your neighborhood. A woman wrote to me last year that she had done just that. She took her kids to each of her neighbor's homes in order to pass out Halloween related Gospel tracks. Her kids did participate in the trick or treating but with a different purpose in mind. She dressed her children in costumes that were completely void of anything evil. She felt it was a very successful evening for her family. If you want to do this, make up your own tracts which would be a meaningful family project. If you don't have the time to create your own, check for Halloween-related tracks at your nearest Christian book store.

For though I am free from all men, I have made myself a slave to all, so that I may win more. To the Jews I became as a Jew, so that I might win Jews; to those who are under the Law, as under the Law though not being myself under the Law, so that I might win those who are under the Law; to those who are without law, as without law, though not being without the law of God but under the law of Christ, so that I might win those who are without law. To the weak I became weak, that I might win the weak; I have become all things to all men, so that I may by all means save some. (I Corinthians 9:19-22)

3. A third alternative is to downplay Halloween and make an effort to substitute Halloween with another celebration. For

instance, designating October 31ˢᵗ as a harvest festival rather than a Halloween celebration could be a first step. Instead of dressing up like figures of evil and death, dress up like men and women of great character or faith. Perhaps over time, Halloween can be undone just as the world is trying to undo Christmas and Easter, as Santa Clause supersedes the birth of Christ, and the Easter bunny supplants the resurrection of Christ.

Behold, I send you out as sheep in the midst of wolves; so be shrewd as serpents and innocent as doves. (Matthew 10:16)

The following verses referenced in this chapter can be found in sequence on my web site, www.tmoments.com. Click on the Book Resources button located on the home page.

Ephesians 6:10-17; Deuteronomy. 18:9-14

TEACHABLE MOMENT 2
THE THANKSGIVING PRESIDENT
(Thanksgiving)

"Thou gave Thy Son to die for me; and hast given me assurance of salvation, upon my repentance and sincerity to conform my life to His holy precepts and example." [1]   *George Washington*

Thanksgiving is one of America's most sacred holidays and began over 200 years ago. George Washington, one of our greatest leaders and Presidents, inaugurated this holiday. He did so because he felt, as a nation, we needed to give God continual gratitude for all He had done to help us gain our freedom and independence.

George Washington certainly gave God His due in his own personal life. By his own statements, he felt God directly and indirectly helped him with every battle he fought, Constitutional amendment he helped pass, and political position he gained.

It is amazing that with all George Washington said in the course of his life, some historians paint George Washington as a Deist. A Deist is one who only accepts God on the basis of nature and reason; one who would not accept the supernatural revelations laid out by Christianity; one who would certainly reject the Bible as God's revelation, and one who would never pray to Christ.[2] Unfortunately, today this is the view taught by so many public schools about George Washington. I was duped into thinking this myself when I attended public school. It was not until I visited Mount Vernon (Washington's home and burial place) with my daughter, Shannon, many years later that I realized how false this view of George Washington was. As I walked from one point to the next around Mount Vernon, I was quite impressed with the words he left behind for all to read, words about God, the Bible, and Jesus Christ. It inspired me to study further and read more about this man who was supposed to be a Deist. Below are some prayers George Washington prayed when he was a young man. Following them is an account of an incredible battle Washington fought when he was only 23 years old. Both his prayers and this battle give a great feel for the kind of faith he had in God.

As you read his prayers, take note of his humility and confidence in God, for such paved the way to greatness, not only during battle, but also as one of the most important Presidents in American history.

Washington's Monday Morning Prayers

"Thou gave Thy Son to die for me; and hast given me assurance of salvation, upon my repentance and sincerity to conform my life to His holy precepts and example. O God, pardon me for Christ's sake, instruct me in the particulars of my duty, and suffer me not to be tempted above what Thou givest me strength to bear. Bless my friends and grant me grace to forgive my enemies as heartily as I desire forgiveness of Thee my heavenly Father."

Washington's Tuesday Prayers

"O blessed Father, let thy Son's blood wash me from all impurities, and cleanse me from the stains of sin that are upon me. Give me grace to lay hold upon His merits; that they may be my conciliation and atonement unto thee that I may know my sins are forgiven, by His death and resurrection." [3]

The Battle of Monongahela (1755)

The Battle of Monongahela, which demanded so much of George's prayerful confidence in a sovereign God, took place during the French and Indian War almost 20 years before the American Revolution; it should have claimed Washington's life. At this time, the colonists were still a part of the British Empire and were engaged with the French and Indians for control of North America. George was a commander under British General George Braddock, who was one of the premier generals in the British army. During this battle Braddock made some critical errors in judgment, and due to them the battle was soundly lost. In order to stop an entire massacre from happening, Washington's responsibility was to cover the retreat. He did such a thorough job that many lives were saved because of his unparalleled wisdom and bravery on the battlefield. Of the 86 officers that sat on horseback, only Washington escaped unharmed with his life. He was the tallest of all the officers and should have been the easiest target to hit. He had two horses shot from underneath him and there were four bullet holes in his coat when the battle concluded, but not a mark on him. What was so defining about Washington was his own assessment of God's sovereignty during the course of this battle. He wrote these words to his brother shortly afterward.

> "As I have heard, since my arrival at this place (Fort Cumberland), a circumstantial account of my death and dying speech, I take this early opportunity of contradicting the first, and of assuring you, that I have not as yet composed the latter. But, by the all–powerful dispensations of God's providence, I have been protected beyond all human probability or expectation; for I had four bullets through my coat, and two horse shot under me, yet escaped unhurt, although death was leveling my companions on every side of me" [4]

The conclusion of the battle left the British General Braddock dead, 714 British killed, 85 out of 86 officers killed or wounded, and 70 out of George Washington's 100 men dead. The enemy (French and Indians) lost 30 soldiers and three officers. It was considered one of the worst defeats in British history. When George arrived home untouched and unharmed, all were impressed, not only his own men, but the British, his family, and even the enemy as well. In fact, the enemy chief who controlled the battle kept track of George for many years afterward. He finally tracked him down 15 years later to let him know what he felt about George and the power of His God.[5] Here is the following account of what this chief said.

> "I am chief and ruler over my tribes. My influence extends to the waters of the great lakes and to the far Blue Mountains. I have traveled a long and weary path that I may see the young warrior of that great battle. It was on the day when the white man's blood mixed with the streams of our forest that I first beheld this chief, George Washington. I called to my young men and said, mark yon tall and daring warrior. He is not of the red coat tribe, he has Indians wisdom, and his warriors fight as we do; himself is alone exposed. Quick let you be certain, and he dies. Our rifles were leveled, rifles which knew not how to miss; was all in vain, a power mightier than we, shielded you. Seeing you were under the special guardianship of the Great Spirit, we immediately ceased to fire at you. I am old and soon shall be gathered to the great council fire of my fathers in the land of shades, but ere I go, there is something bids me speak in the voice of prophecy. Listen! The Great Spirit protects that man (pointing

at Washington), and guides his destinies; he will become the chief of nations, and a people yet unborn will hail him as the founder of a mighty empire. I am come to pay homage to the man who is the particular favorite of Heaven, and who can never die in battle." [6] (Washington began fighting for his country six years later.)

I love reading this account, as I am sure you did; much of what the chief said turned out to be true. It is too bad this chief put his confidence in a great spirit, as he called him, because according to the Scripture there is no great spirit (Indian or otherwise) that can bring anyone into the kingdom of God other than Jesus Christ. *(John 14:6; John 3:16-18)* My hope is that this chief continued to follow Washington's life and testimony and finally realized Jesus Christ as his own personal savior.

Teachable Moment

Before you lift a fork at your Thanksgiving celebration, read this story of Washington's battle at *Monongahela* to your family. Ask them what they think of it, especially in respect to his great courage. Then read George's two prayers, along with his official Thanksgiving Proclamation recorded below. If you find the Old English difficult to read, then rewrite it in your own words. Have your children help in the rewriting if they are old enough.

After all is read, have each in your family share an experience where God protected or guided them in a special way that only He could have done. Then, finish by praying for the same humility and confidence George Washington demonstrated in his life. Such a prayer, I believe, can be the greatest thanks at Thanksgiving you can give God for all He's done for you. Then, eat away!

On a last note, here is how I rewrote George's prayers; it might help you in rewriting yours.

Washington's Monday Morning Prayer
(Revised)

"Lord, thank you for giving me Your Son to die for me. I recognize that this gift of salvation was given to me through my repentance and sincere desire to follow Your Word. Lord, forgive me once again for any trespasses for Christ's sake, and teach me in every detail of the duties of my life. Help me to overcome all temptation, and allow me only to bear what I can.

Bless all of my friends and grant me the grace to forgive even my enemies as heartily as I desire your daily forgiveness in the sins I commit."

Washington's Tuesday prayers
(Revised)

"Oh Lord, let the blood of Christ cleanse me from all my sins. May there not be even a stain left when You are through. Give me the grace to lay hold of the works you have planned for me in my lifetime. I pray Lord that all will see the evidence of my transformation, a man who has been forgiven."

Washington's Thanksgiving Day Declaration
(October 3, 1789)

"Whereas, it is the duty of all nations to acknowledge the sovereignty of almighty God, to obey His will, to be grateful for His benefits, and humbly to implore His protection and favor; and, whereas both Houses of Congress have, by their joint committee, requested me to recommend to the people of the United States a day of public thanksgiving and prayer, to be observed by acknowledging with grateful hearts the many and signal favors (signs) of Almighty God, especially to establish a form of government for their safety and happiness. Now, therefore, I do recommend and assign Thursday, the 26th day of November to be devoted by the people of these States to be the service of that great and glorious Being (God), who is the Benefit Author (Creator) of all the good that was, that is, or will be." [7]

The following verses referenced in this chapter can be found in sequence on my web site, www.tmoments.com. Click on the Book Resources button located on the home page.

John 14:6; John 3:16-18.

TEACHABLE MOMENT 3
COLORS AND SYMBOLS OF CHRISTMAS
(Christmas)

But the angel said to them, "Do not be afraid; for behold, I bring you good news of great joy which will be for all the people; for today in the city of David there has been born for you a Savior, who is Christ the Lord. This will be a sign for you: you will find a baby wrapped in cloths and lying in a manger." And suddenly there appeared with the angel a multitude of the heavenly host praising God and saying, "Glory to God in the highest."
(Luke 2:10-14)

There is so much materialism built into Christmas that the message of Christ is often lost each year. Sadly, the birth of Christ, the Savior of mankind, is often substituted with the coming of Santa, the setting up of the tree, and the giving of gifts. Needless to say, the story of Santa can never replace the birth of the Savior, but Santa's story and the other "worldly" traditions of our present day Christmas are not without spiritual merit or beginnings.

The modern mythical Santa Claus, for example, developed from the real person Saint Nicholas. According to tradition, Saint Nicholas was the youngest and one of the kindest bishops in the early church. He started the Christmas tradition of giving presents to deserving children in 300 A.D. in the town of Myra, Turkey. It was his intention to reward well-behaved children for their accomplishments and Christmas was the perfect time, since it was the yearly celebration of the greatest gift ever given mankind, the gift of the Savior, Jesus Christ. Children loved Saint Nicholas and his habit of bringing gifts so much that the custom continued and even developed in other countries. The name St. Nicholas later changed to Santy, or Santa Claus.[1,2,3]

Teachable Moment

Since it is difficult to escape the worldly impact on Christmas, it is imperative to give your children a spiritual set of glasses through which to view this God-sent time. In order to carry this out, teach your children the meaning of the Christmas symbols and colors.

The star

Teach your children that the star was the heavenly sign of promise long ago. God promised a Savior for the world and the star was the sign of the fulfillment of this promise. The countless shining stars at night, one for each man, now show the burning hope of all mankind. *(Matthew 2:2)*

The color red

Teach your children that red is the first color of Christmas. It was first used by the faithful people to remind them of the blood which was shed by the Savior for all people. Christ gave His life and shed His blood that every man might have God's gift of eternal life. Red is deep, intense, and vivid; it is the greatest color of all. It is the symbol of the gift of God. *(I Peter 1:17-19; Revelation 1:5)*

> *While they were eating, Jesus took some bread, and after a blessing, He broke it and gave it to the disciples, and said, "Take, eat; this is My body." And when He had taken a cup and given thanks, He gave it to them, saying, "Drink from it, all of you; for this is My blood of the covenant, which is poured out for many for forgiveness of sins." (Matthew 26:26-28)*

The green tree

The pure green color of the stately fir tree remains green all year round. This depicts life eternal in heaven. Green is the youthful, hopeful, and abundant color of nature. All the needles point heavenward, which symbolizes man's thoughts toward heaven. The great green tree has been man's best friend. It has sheltered him, warmed him, and made beauty for him.

> *He who has an ear, let him hear what the Spirit says to the churches. To him who overcomes, I will grant to eat of the tree of life which is in the Paradise of God. (Revelation 2:7)*

The bell

Teach your children that as the lost sheep are found by the sound of the bell, the bell should ring for man to return to the fold of God's arms. The bell further signifies that all are precious in the eyes of the Lord, because He wants us to always return to Him.

The Lord is not slow about His promise, as some count slowness, but is patient toward you, not wishing for any to perish but for all to come to repentance. (II Peter 3:9)

The candle

Teach your children that the candle shows man's gratitude for the star of long ago. Its small light is the mirror of starlight. At first, candles were placed on the trees like many glowing stars shining against the dark green. Colored lights are often used today, but should still remind us of the original star that heralded Christ's birth.

When they saw the star, they rejoiced exceedingly with great joy. After coming into the house they saw the Child with Mary His mother; and they fell to the ground and worshiped Him. Then, opening their treasures, they presented to Him gifts of gold, frankincense, and myrrh. (Matthew 2:10-11)

The bow

A bow is placed on a present to remind us of the tie we have with God and other believers.

Therefore I, the prisoner of the Lord, implore you to walk in a manner worthy of the calling with which you have been called, with all humility and gentleness, with patience, showing tolerance for one another in love, being diligent to preserve the unity of the Spirit in the bond of peace. There is one body and one Spirit, just as also you were called in one hope of your calling; one Lord, one faith, one baptism, one God and Father of all who is over all and through all and in all. (Ephesians 4:1-6)

The candy cane

Teach your children that the candy cane represents the shepherd's crook. The crook on the staff helps bring back the strayed sheep to the flock. The candy cane represents God's great love as He rescued us unto Himself. It also represents the helping hand we should show at Christmas time, as well as the symbol of being our brother's keeper. *(Psalm 23:4; I Peter 5:2)*

> *...but through love serve one another. For the whole Law is fulfilled in one word, in the statement, "You shall love your neighbor as yourself." (Galatians 5:13-14)*

The wreath

Teach your children the wreath symbolizes God's eternal love for us all, it never ceases, stops, or ends. It is one continuous circle of godly affection for us all.

> *Who will separate us from the love of Christ? Will tribulation, or distress, or persecution, or famine, or nakedness, or peril, or sword? For I am convinced that neither death, nor life, nor angels, nor principalities, nor things present, nor things to come, nor powers, nor height, nor depth, nor any other created thing, will be able to separate us from the love of God, which is in Christ Jesus our Lord. (Romans 8:35, 38-39)*

Finally, to carry out this Teachable Moment, pick an evening before Christmas to share this symbolism with your children. As you sit down in front of the Christmas tree together, ask your children to point out or gather up the objects they see in your home that are represented above. As you conclude, pray a prayer of great praise, and then give your children a candy cane as a memento of God's great love for them and our need to love others.

The following verses referenced in this chapter can be found in sequence on my web site, www.tmoments.com. Click on the Book Resources button located on the home page.

Matthew 2: 22; I Peter I: 17: 17-19; Revelation 1:5-6; Psalm 23:4; I Peter 5: 2

TEACHABLE MOMENT 4
THE STAR OF BETHLEHEM

(Christmas)

When they saw the star, they rejoiced exceedingly with great joy.
(Matthew 2:10)

The star of Bethlehem is one of the most fascinating events of the first Christmas. The star had tremendous significance then and still should today. Before sharing this epoch story of the star, let me share with you what Christmas is not. It is not shopping for gifts until you are exhausted, nor is it rushing from one store to the next for a bargain sale. Sad to say, this is what Christmas has turned out to be for too many, which is tragic in more ways than one. Perhaps one of the most tragic occurrences happened in New York a number of years ago when a temporary Christmas worker was killed by a throng of stampeding shoppers. I saw this story on the T.V. news one evening and couldn't believe what I heard. Evidently, a big department store announced a huge sale on some big items right before Christmas. In order to purchase them, shoppers had to be at the store when it opened. So they lined up the next morning, and when the doors opened, they stampeded, running over a young worker in their way. He was crushed to death, even though some of his fellow workers tried to rescue him. The store was immediately closed, which drew the ire of many shoppers who still wanted to shop. Needless to say, these shoppers forgot the true meaning of Christmas, which did not start with a bargain sale, but a great star in the sky.

According to Matthew's gospel, great wise men (how many is unknown) from the East came bearing three gifts to the Christ child 20 centuries ago. Inspired by a spectacular moving star, they set out on at least a two year journey that eventually led them to Bethlehem, the birthplace of Christ. *(Matthew 2:1-2)* When they arrived, they immediately recognized that Jesus was born to be the Savior of the world. Through an omniscient and sovereign God, these men worshipped Jesus without hesitation when they found Him. How was it possible for these men who lived so far from Israel (God's chosen center of evangelism) to find this path to their own salvation via a moving star? Could such a star that moved continuously from one part of the world to the other even exist? And if so, what does this tell our children (God's future church) today about His desire to use them as His guiding stars to reach their generation with the message of salvation? (I Timothy 2:3-4)

Historically speaking, and without much argument, the star of Bethlehem actually existed around the time of Jesus' birth. According to astronomical records, a remarkable conjunction of planets and stars (Jupiter and Saturn and the constellation Pisces) that occurs only once every eight hundred years, took place two years previous to the birth of Christ. It is ascertained by several Christian scholars that this planet/star cluster was perhaps the first sign that initiated the wise men's sojourn to Bethlehem. It was an extraordinary, brilliant spectacle in the night sky; everyone in the East would have taken note of it. In the year following, planet Mars joined this constellation. As a result, these three planets (Jupiter, Saturn, Mars) joined together appearing as an extraordinary effervescent star. This conjunction of planets took place over Jerusalem right before the birth of Jesus. The final movement of the Bethlehem star from Jerusalem to Bethlehem (the night of Jesus' birth) was, according to the Chinese astronomers of the day, like a purpose-driven meteor.[1]

Personally, I love the way these planet/star clusters noted by the historians and Christian scholars collaborated much of Matthew's account concerning the star of Bethlehem. Although, whether God used His own created star system or a miraculous single star 2000 years ago to bring the wise men to Bethlehem matters little, because His overall plan was to highlight the birth of Jesus, the Messiah. (John 6:44; John 1:1-4, 9) As to whether their faith preceded their journey to Bethlehem or culminated at its end is not known, but there is little doubt these wise men believed in Jesus as their Savior at one time or the other.

> *After coming into the house they saw the Child with Mary His mother; and they fell to the ground and worshiped Him. Then, opening their treasures, they presented to Him gifts of gold, frankincense, and myrrh. (Matthew 2:11)*

When they concluded their worship, they returned home. During their journey back, the light of a guiding star was not needed. The star that led them to Bethlehem was not the same light that brought them home. That light was the inward light they received when they put their faith in God's provision for their salvation, Jesus Christ, the Son of God. Thirty years later, Jesus Himself would state to those who put their trust in Him as the Son of God, "You are the light of the world, a city set on a hill." *(Matthew 5:14)* The wise men returned home with this light; they were God's first missionaries to the East after the birth of Christ.

Your children, upon believing and receiving Christ as Savior, are now the wise men of their generation. *(John 1:12)* They, like the wise men, are the stars of light that will lead many of their own generation to salvation.

Teachable Moment

In this Teachable Moment, take your children outside on Christmas Eve for a time of reflection. As you look at the sky, pretend that one of the stars is the one of Bethlehem that led the wise men to the manger. Be sure to have your Bible with you and a flash light, if necessary. As each of your children look up at the star, read Matthew 2:1-11 about the star of that day and the wise men. When you are finished reading, tell your children that they are like the stars of Bethlehem, because they are a light to the world that can guide their friends and neighbors to salvation.

When you return inside, sit down with your children in front of your Christmas tree. Ask them how they could better lead others to Christ by being God's guiding light. Then, go outside again with your children and walk around your neighborhood. Pick a number of houses over which to stop and pray. Pray that the families in these homes will one day receive Christ as Lord. *(Acts 4:31)*

When you have completed your walk, challenge your children to continue to pray for those in these homes. Over the years, make this a tradition at Christmas Eve and add a little to it just as you add new ornaments to your tree each year. Perhaps, next year you can send these neighbors a Christmas card with the message of the manger.

The following verses referenced in this chapter can be found in sequence on my web site, www.tmoments.com. Click on the Book Resources button located on the home page.

Matthew 2:1-2; I Timothy 2:3-4; John 6:44; John 1:1-4; 9; Matthew 5:14; John 1:12; Acts 4:31

TEACHABLE MOMENT 5
RESOLUTIONS
(New Year's Eve)

Therefore if anyone is in Christ, he is a new creature; the old things passed away; behold, new things have come.
(II Corinthians 5:17)

New Year's Day arrives with many traditions like football games, parades, and, for some, forgettable parties. It also marks the day we do our best to make a quick review of the way we lived our lives during the past year. In response, we usually make New Year's resolutions, announcing either to others or just ourselves the changes we will make. Unfortunately, by February, for most of us, these resolutions have started to go by the way side. By March, we are back to our old ways of living, even as Christians.

The reason for this inability to change is lack of "how to," inadequate knowledge, and need for power. After a time most of us realize we possess all of these inadequacies and God readily agrees with us. This is why He gave us the Scriptures and His accompanying power, so that we would know what to do and have the power to do it. The first part is easy, all you have to do is pick up the Scriptures and begin reading. The second is more difficult, because it calls on you to trust Him to carry out within you what you have read. You do this by asking Him to help you through prayer, and then believing He will through faith. If you ask through prayer and believe with faith, whatever resolutions you have set for yourself this year will be realized. God guarantees it.

All Scripture is inspired by God and profitable for teaching, for reproof, for correction, for training in righteousness; so that the man of God may be adequate, equipped for every good work. (II Timothy 3:16-17)

Trust in the Lord with all your heart and do not lean on your own understanding. In all your ways acknowledge Him, and He will make your paths straight. (Proverbs 3:5-6)

The following are some Scriptures to read and reflect on during this next year. They fit most situations and conditions; start with them! But don't forget to humbly ask for His help all along the way.

When in sorrow	(John 14)
How to be right with God	(John 3:16, Romans 3:22-24, Romans 5:8-11, Revelations 3:19-20)
When others fail you	(Psalm 27)
If you have been unfruitful	(John 15)
If you have sinned	(Psalm 51)
If you worry	(Matthew 6:19-34)
If you are in danger	(Psalm 91)
When God seems far away	(Psalm 139)
When your faith needs stirring	(Hebrews 11)
When you are lonely and fearful	(Psalm 23)
When you are bitter or critical	(I Corinthians 13)
When you want to experience true happiness	(Colossians 3:12-17)
When you feel down and out	(Romans 8:31)
When you want peace and rest	(Matthew 11:28-30)
When the world seems bigger than God	(Psalm 90)
When you want assurance of your faith	(Romans 8:1-30)
When you want courage for the task	(Joshua 1)
When you want to know how to get along with others	(Romans 12)

If you are depressed	*(Psalm 27)*
When you are financially strapped	*(Psalm 37)*
When you are the recipient of unkindness	*(John 15)*
When you get discouraged at work	*(Psalm 126)*
When you are scared	*(Psalm 34:7)*
When you are feeling insecure	*(Psalm 121)*
When you need reassurance	*(Psalm 145:18)*
When you feel crushed	*(Psalm 34:18)*

Teachable Moment

During New Years, gather your family together for a time of reflection. Encourage your children to write down the changes they would like to make for the coming year. As they do, also mention the changes you would like to make; you don't want them to do anything you aren't willing to do, too. Afterward, take them to your family car in the garage and ask them to make every effort to move that car out of the garage. When they ask for the keys to start the engine, tell them you lost them, and they will have to move it without the keys. Hopefully, they will look at you a bit puzzled and say something like, "This car can't be moved without the engine turned on." They may even exclaim, "Where will the power come from to move the car?" Applaud them for their insight, and agree that the car cannot move without the keys to turn it on. And then tell them that neither can they make the changes they want to make next year, unless they have God's keys, which are the Scriptures and His power to accomplish it. Conclude, that for the next several weeks, to get everyone started on their resolutions, the entire family will begin reading and reflecting on some of the 26 situations and conditions listed previously with their corresponding Scripture. If you do this, there likely won't be as many resolutions to make next year on January 1st. And praise God for that!

Note: Scriptures within this article are not listed on web site.

TEACHABLE MOMENT 6
LINCOLN THE CHRISTIAN
(President's Day)

"We have been the recipients of the choicest bounties of heaven. We have been preserved these many years in peace and prosperity. We have grown in numbers, wealth and power as no other nation has ever grown. But we have forgotten God. It behooves us then to humble ourselves before the offended powers, to confess our national sins and to pray for clemency and forgiveness." [1]
Abraham Lincoln

In the month of February each year, as a nation we have often celebrated two holidays commemorating the birthdays of George Washington and Abraham Lincoln. That has changed somewhat in the last several years, as Lincoln's birthday has been replaced by President's Day. Only a few states still take a holiday specifically in honor of him, but regardless, he still remains one of our greatest Presidents because he kept our nation together at a very critical time, and did away with the awful institution of slavery.

Before Lincoln became President, he wasn't very successful in much that he tried, whether in business or politics. In 1832, at age 22, he failed in business. During the same year. he ran for the legislature and was defeated. In 1833, he failed in business again. In 1836, he suffered a nervous breakdown. In 1838, he lost in an effort to become Speaker of the House in the Illinois State Legislature. Five years later, he ran for Congress but lost. In 1846, he ran for Congress and won, and then lost his re-election bid in 1848. He ran for the U.S. Senate in 1854 and lost. He ran for the Vice-Presidential nomination in 1856 and lost. Once more, he ran for a Senate seat in 1858 and lost. Finally, in 1860, he amazingly became the 16th President of the United States.[2]

Like Lincoln's early business and political career, his relationship with God also started off rather poorly; hardly existent at times. "Drifting" best describes his early years as a boy and young man when it came to God and His Word. "Questioning" reflects Lincoln's spiritual thoughts in his early 20s and "religious indifference" depicts his late 20s and 30s. During Lincoln's 40s he put forth some serious doubts about God and the Bible.

However when he became President and the Civil War began, Lincoln gradually had a change of heart. For the first time in his life, he started showing evidence of a real faith in God and Christ. Then in his last years, as the Civil War wound down, Lincoln's belief in God and Christ soared.[3]

> *"When I left Springfield I asked the people to pray for me. I was not a Christian. When I buried my son, the severest trial of my life, I was not a Christian. But when I went to Gettysburg and saw the graves of thousands of our solders. I then and there consecrated myself to Christ. Yes, I do love Jesus."*[4]

For decades though, historians refused to believe Abraham Lincoln ever embraced Christianity. They felt he only used Christian words and phrases to advance his political causes. Perhaps, this was due to his earlier questioning, indifference, and expressed doubts about God and the Bible. But in the second year of his Presidency, Lincoln made a very clear profession of faith. During this critical year, the second year of the Civil War, Lincoln suffered greatly. His Union Army suffered one loss after the next. The mounting criticism he received for these losses was unbearable. He was termed by many of the press on both sides of the conflict as America's worst President. Along with all of these events, his beloved son Willie died. Yet, in his hours of agony, he dedicated his life to God and openly confessed his love for Jesus.[5] *(Romans 10:9-11)*

After his commitment to God, the war began to gradually change; Lee lost a huge battle at Gettysburg for the South and eventually surrendered at Appomattox. As the war drew to a close, Lincoln went from being reported the worst President to being the best, which was very typical of the media back then. All of this mattered little to Lincoln; his newfound relationship with Christ was everything to him. On the way to Ford's theatre, the last day of his life, he talked of going to Jerusalem to walk where Jesus walked; that evening, he did just that.[6]

Therefore, when the celebration of President's Day comes, remember the commitment Lincoln made to God, along with other American Presidents who have made Christ their Lord. I leave you with some of Lincoln words, delivered on March 30th, 1863, when proclaiming a national day of fasting for our nation.

> *"...whereas, it is the duty of nations as well as of men to own their dependence upon the over-ruling power of God; to confess their sins and transgressions in humble sorrow, yet with; assured hope that genuine repentance will lead to*

mercy and pardon; and to recognize the sublime truth, announced in the Holy Scriptures and proven by all history, that those nations only are blessed who God is the Lord.." [7]

Teachable Moment

In this Teachable Moment, there are two possible applications to consider. The first one is to take out a five-dollar bill and have your children study its features. Ask them to identify which President is on the bill. When they have identified Lincoln, remind them of the love and commitment he had for God. Then ask them to find words on the bill that relate to his commitment to God and Christ. Those words are: "In God We Trust," which is exactly what Lincoln did with his faith at the end of his life.

The second consideration is more involved and is best carried out when your children hit their later elementary years and beyond. In this Teachable Moment, study the spiritual life of Lincoln together with your children. There are several good books to help with this, like: *Abraham Lincoln* by David Collins and *Abraham Lincoln the Christian* by William J. Johnson. You can find both on the internet. Afterwards, help them prepare a speech to be presented either at church or school if possible. I did this with my daughter which really turned out well and has stuck in her memory ever since. Here is a portion of Shannon's speech which was spoken at her sixth grade graduation.

Abraham Lincoln: A Man After God's Heart
By Shannon McClain

"Many fugitive slaves fighting for the North during the Civil War were overcome with joy when their freedom was declared through the Emancipation Proclamation. This perhaps was the greatest day in these slaves' lives, because of one of the greatest Presidents in the United States history. Of course, the man of whom I speak is Abraham Lincoln. From the very beginning of this man's life, he would say many things to change lives and turn a nation around.

Last year, when I recited the Gettysburg Address in class, I admired many things Lincoln said. "That these men shall not die in vain" sticks in my memory especially after visiting Gettysburg. But the words that I will never forget were sitting next to Lincoln at the Lincoln Memorial. "That these truths are self-

evident that all men are created equal." I believe that the words he said here and his forcefulness to put an end to slavery were his greatest contributions to this country.

Why was he so wise, so bold, so honest, and such a great man? Lincoln was because he had three great characteristics that led his life. Three characteristics I can hopefully learn to use in my life: compassion, honesty, and his love for God.

Lincoln was a man of compassion, because he felt and responded to the hurt and sufferings of others. His compassion drove him to free all men and women through the Emancipation Proclamation. But his compassion ran deeper than just being a great lawmaker. Lincoln on many occasions was found teaching the White House black servants to read and to understand the written language and he ended each session with prayer for their needs.[8]

Lincoln was known as "Honest Abe." He kept his word to the black slaves of this nation by freeing them as he said he would. Lincoln was also honest with himself about how these events happened. One day as Lincoln was traveling by boat to Richmond, many slaves caught sight of him and began yelling! "Here is the great Messiah! He has come to free us all." But "Honest Abe" told them that it was God, and God alone, that brought them their freedom.[9]

Lincoln respected God, but it wasn't until the death of his son and the bloody battle of Gettysburg that he dedicated his life to Christ. In his own words, he said, "I love Jesus." [10]

We honor Lincoln today by putting his picture on our currency and naming cities after him. But for me the greatest honor was given to him the last day of his life, the day he went to Ford's theatre. According to his wife, this was the happiest day of his life. After Lee had surrendered, Lincoln knew the war was over and he spoke of the things he would like to do most. Lincoln wanted to visit Jerusalem and walk where Jesus walked.[11] That night, a shot rang out, and the 16th President of the United States walked with Jesus in Paradise with believers who gave him the parade he missed on earth." (Revelation 21:1-2)

The following verses referenced in this chapter can be found in sequence on my web site, www.tmoments.com. Click on the Book Resources button located on the home page.

Romans 10:9-11; Revelation 21:1-2

TEACHABLE MOMENT 7
ALL IS LOST: ALL IS RESTORED
(Easter)

Behold, I am the LORD, the God of all flesh; is anything too difficult for Me?
(Jeremiah 32:27)

This Easter article is one of the more intriguing I have written; it is based on Scripture I have wanted to explore for years. The Teachable Moment, "All is Lost, All is Restored" deals with an unusual occurrence during Jesus' crucifixion and resurrection – one on which few Bible commentators explore to any extent. I will attempt to interpret and apply Matthew 27:51-54. It is one of the most incredible Scriptures I have read.

Earthquakes were very common in Israel in Jesus' day, much like they are in Southern California where I grew up. Thus, when two earthquakes hit Jerusalem during His crucifixion and resurrection, it most likely did not surprise the Jews. The only ones who might have been caught off guard by such seismic activity were the Roman soldiers who were new to the region. However, regardless of whether you were a Jew or a Roman, earthquakes did cause fear and got everyone's attention.

I know because my wife and I have been through most of the recent California earthquakes. Two of the worst took place in 1971 and 1994; both of us were scared to death and caught off guard when they occurred. In 1971, the San Fernando/Sylmar earthquake killed 65 people and caused over 50 million dollars of damage. In 1994, the Northridge earthquake killed 57 people and 15 billion dollars of damage resulted. In the Northridge earthquake, everything in our house was either shattered or broken to some extent. My wife and daughter slept outside in our van for a week until the aftershocks subsided. My son and I braved it out in the house; isn't that what guys do?

As frightening and attention-getting as those earthquakes were in Jerusalem over 2,000 years ago, there was another event even more startling that took place, and I am not talking about Jesus' resurrection. Matthew is the only Gospel writer to record this astonishing event as he may have been the only one to see it firsthand. Regardless, it is in the Scripture and plays a significant part in the events of Jesus' death and resurrection. As you read the following verses, take note that the first verse about the veil of the Temple was in each of the other Gospels. It is only included here to give context.

> *And behold, the veil of the temple was torn in two from top to bottom; and the earth shook and the rocks were split. The tombs were opened, and many bodies of the saints who had fallen asleep were raised; and coming out of the tombs after His resurrection they entered the holy city and appeared to many. Now the centurion, and those who were with him keeping guard over Jesus, when they saw the earthquake and the things that were happening, became very frightened and said, "Truly this was the Son of God!" (Matthew 27:51-54)*

Who were these saints? What was God's purpose in raising them from the dead? Where were they before their bodies were raised from the dead? What did they do for three days before entering Jerusalem after Jesus' resurrection? How long did they live before dying again? These are all challenging questions, but I'll do my best to answer them according to my knowledge of the times and the Bible.

Who were these Saints and what was their purpose?

A few Bible commentators purport that these saints were some of the earlier Patriarchs, men like Moses and Elijah. After all, these two showed up at the Mount of Transfiguration; why not again in order to accomplish God's purpose? But, I don't believe so, for no one in Jerusalem would have recognized them. There were no previous portraits or pictures from which to identify them.

In respect to God's purpose in raising these saints from the dead, I construe they were believers in Christ who had recently died. They were men, women, and even children who would have been recognizable when they walked through Jerusalem after Jesus' resurrection. This works well into God's purpose, which I believe was to give Jerusalem further evidence that Jesus had truly risen from the dead, in the same way as those who stood before them.

Where were the saints before their bodies were raised from the dead?

The Scripture is pretty clear about where believers go when they die, whether that is in the Old Testament times, Jesus' day, or today; all are immediately in the presence of God. In our culture, we use the term "pass on" for death to soften the blow. In Jesus' time they used the term "fallen asleep." No matter the term, when believers die they are with God, just as Moses and Elijah were when they appeared to Jesus, James, John, and Peter at the Mount of Transfiguration. *(Matthew 17:1-9; Luke 23:39-43)*

Therefore, being always of good courage, and knowing that while we are at home in the body we are absent from the Lord, for we walk by faith, not by sight. And we are of good courage, I say, and prefer rather to be absent from the body and to be at home with the Lord. (II Corinthians 5:6 -8)

But we do not want you to be uninformed, brethren, about those who are asleep, so that you will not grieve as do the rest who have no hope. For if we believe that Jesus died and rose again, even so God will bring with Him those who have fallen asleep in Jesus. (I Thessalonians 4:13-14)

What did the risen saints do before entering Jerusalem?

Although there is no way of really knowing what they did after being raised from the dead until they entered Jerusalem, it can be assumed they went home and showed themselves first to their own families and friends. What a joyous surprise that must have been for those mothers, fathers, brothers, and sisters. After three days at home, they fulfilled God's plan and entered Jerusalem showing themselves to all. In the midst of such an obvious miracle, it seems almost impossible they would not have proclaimed a risen Christ during their walk around that great city. For what other purpose were they raised except to do that?

How long did the saints live before dying again?

Once again, there is no direct Scriptural reference detailing how long they lived before dying again. The only Scripture to draw from is John 11 where Lazarus had a similar experience. He, like these saints, died and was raised from the dead. Lazarus' raising was done because of Jesus' great compassion and love for him and his family, as well as building belief in Jesus and His coming resurrection. How long Lazarus lived afterward is not known, nor is it anymore important than it was for the saints. In both cases,

I surmise that there were a lot fewer tears at their second funerals than the first because all those attending their funerals would know, as never before, that life doesn't end on earth but goes on in a glorious way with God and others throughout eternity.

> *Jesus said, "Remove the stone." Martha, the sister of the deceased, said to Him, "Lord, by this time there will be a stench, for he has been dead four days." Jesus said to her, "Did I not say to you that if you believe, you will see the glory of God?" So they removed the stone. Then Jesus raised His eyes, and said, "Father, I thank You that You have heard Me. I knew that You always hear Me; but because of the people standing around I said it, so that they may believe that You sent Me." When He had said these things, He cried out with a loud voice, "Lazarus, come forth." The man who had died came forth, bound hand and foot with wrappings, and his face was wrapped around with a cloth. Jesus said to them, "Unbind him, and let him go." Therefore many of the Jews who came to Mary, and saw what He had done, believed in Him. (John 11:39-45)*

Final Thoughts

As you celebrate this Easter amidst perhaps a very difficult and precarious time where many have recently lost their jobs, savings, and homes, God is still making miracles. Two thousand years ago, the Jewish people had lost everything; the Roman occupation had wiped them out; many were living from one meal to the next. Then, Christ came and things began to change. For the first time in years, they had hope and a renewed expectation that God would restore their lives and their nation, but at the height of their hope, Jesus was crucified. All was lost! All was lost! All was lost!

After Jesus' body was torn down from the cross, all returned to their homes, likely head down, broken, and downtrodden. All of a sudden, for some (perhaps those who had held onto their faith), loved ones who had recently died began showing up at their doorsteps. With tears joyously rolling down their cheeks, how many ways did they say, "How can this be? How can this be?" But it was, because when God is in charge, anything is possible. At the height of their despair, God sent two great miracles, one of the risen saints and the other of Jesus Himself. The saints brought more evidence of Jesus, and Jesus brought victory over death and sin, and the promise of eternal life to all who believe.

All was restored, all was restored, and all was restored! Is He not still restoring today those who put their trust in Him?

O death, where is your victory? O death, where is your sting? The sting of death is sin,.. but thanks be to God, who gives us the victory through our Lord Jesus Christ. Therefore, my beloved brethren, be steadfast, immovable, always abounding in the work of the Lord... (I Corinthians 15:55-58)

Teachable Moment

In this Teachable Moment, show your children some pictures of loved ones in your family who have passed on to be with the Lord. Talk about them, particularly in respect to their faith in God and how much you love and miss them. Then, read and tell your children the account of the saints at Jesus' resurrection. Tell your children that if this happened to you today rather than to those in Jerusalem 2000 years ago, you would have been equally as thrilled to see your loved ones showing up fully restored and praising God. Consequently, from here on, when anyone in your family runs across a picture of a loved one who has passed on, let it remind them of those saints in Jerusalem who were restored to life so that all might believe in Jesus and His resurrection.

The following verses referenced in this chapter can be found in sequence on my web site, www.tmoments.com. Click on the Book Resources button located on the home page.

Matthew 17: 1-9; Luke 23: 39-43

TEACHABLE MOMENT 8
SILENT SATURDAY

(Easter)

*My soul waits in silence for God only; from Him is my salvation.
(Psalm 62: 1)*

Too often when we remember the events of Easter week, we tend to make a leap from Good Friday to Easter Sunday; straight from the crucifixion to the resurrection. We skip right over what I call *Silent Saturday*. I don't know why this is so; perhaps, it is because there is more biblical material supporting the events around Good Friday and Resurrection Sunday or maybe because these two dramatic events are so intense and spectacular, we don't hear the message of *Silent Saturday*.

As Christians, we often know how to accept the tragedy of Good Friday and look forward to the victory of Resurrection Sunday, but struggle with waiting for things to change, which *Silent Saturday* represents. Simply said, we don't like the in-between times in life where we must wait, wait, and then wait some more. The meaning of *Silent Saturday* is rarely taught during Easter week, but it should be as the message is empowering. Nevertheless, before we look at this message, let's briefly revisit the wonder of Good Friday and Resurrection Sunday.

Good Friday reminds us of many remarkable things, the most important of which is the fact that Jesus died for our sins. He laid them all on the cross and took care of them, so we could have a forever relationship with Him. *(Romans 3:23; John 3:16; Colossians 2:14)* All we need to do is repent of our sins and believe in Him as Lord and Savior. *(Mark 1:14-15)* Without His supreme sacrifice, we would all be lost and separated from God and His loving grace forever. Perhaps this is why Good Friday is called Good Friday; it was totally for our good.

The second message of Good Friday, a practical everyday application, is that the worst has happened and the best is yet to come just around the corner. Even though the "Good Fridays" in our lives may be tough and sometimes unbearable, God promises they will pass. *(II Corinthians 4:7-12, 17-18)* He promises that He will bring peace to every circumstance in our lives whether it is realized here on earth or in heaven. *(II Corinthians 5:2, 6, 7-9)*

SILENT SATURDAY

Resurrection Sunday is the most joyously celebrated day of all; churches across the world pack out their auditoriums, worship centers, and meeting places on this day. The very fact that Jesus rose from the dead, as He said He would, brings all of us who believe in Him a real sense of peace and joy. *(Luke 24:1-6)* Since He did this, He can do anything, even bring a miracle to our own lives if need be.

Silent Saturday is rarely the focus; it is an in-between day where nothing is seemingly going on with Jesus. Correspondingly, it represents the days we spend waiting for God to get us from our "Good Friday" circumstances to "Resurrection Sundays". During these times of waiting, we often wonder whether God is really working in our lives.

What was Jesus doing on the Saturday between Good Friday and Resurrection Sunday? If we can answer this, perhaps we can have a better feel for those seemingly *Silent Saturdays* that come. First, He did not stay on the cross long like many others who were crucified by the Romans. He was immediately taken to a tomb. According to Scripture, His body stayed in the tomb in a state of death until early Sunday morning. *(Mark 16:9)* But even though Jesus' body stayed in the tomb until Resurrection Sunday, His spirit did not. Some time shortly after He had been wrapped in linen clothes, sprinkled with the traditional burial myrrh, and shut in by a sealed stone door, Jesus' spirit got up and left His body. *(John 19:39; John 20: 6-9)* His leaving could have been a matter of a few hours, a single hour, or even just a few minutes, but He did leave! Where did He go and what did He do during that time between Good Friday and Resurrection Sunday? To begin with, He was not on earth, but with those who were in hell, with those who had rejected God's plan of salvation. He was there preaching the Gospel, sharing with them who He was and working as always for the kingdom of God.

> *For Christ also died for sins once for all, the just for the unjust, so that He might bring us to God, having been put to death in the flesh, but made alive in the spirit; in which also He went and made proclamation to the spirits now in prison. (I Peter 3:18-19)*

> *But to each one of us grace was given according to the measure of Christ's gift. Therefore it says, When He ascended on high, He led captive a host of captives, and He gave gifts to men. Now this expression, He ascended, what does it mean except that He also had descended into the lower parts of the earth? He who*

descended is Himself also He who ascended far above all the heavens, so that He might fill all things. (Ephesians 4:7-9)

Where can I go from Your Spirit? Or where can I flee from Your presence? If I ascend to heaven, You are there; If I make my bed in Sheol, behold, You are there. (Psalm 139:7-8)

Why did He do this; why did he go to hell to preach? They were already lost; it was too late for them. I don't know for sure. Perhaps even those who are lost forever deserve a right to finally see who Jesus was and what they missed out on by not repenting and believing as they should. The Scripture tells us that every knee shall bow and every tongue will confess that Jesus Christ is Lord, so maybe this was the reason. *(Romans 14:11)* Whatever the reason, the point is that on the Saturday between Good Friday and Resurrection Sunday, Jesus was working hard to get His will accomplished for you, me, and every person who has ever lived. When *Silent Saturdays* come in your life, realize God is hard at work getting things ready so that when your Resurrection Sunday comes, you will be ready. *(Psalm 121:1-3)* Instead of pouting or saying woe is me during these times, do all you can to bolster your faith as you wait.

Teachable Moment

For this Teachable Moment, pick a Saturday near Easter or, if possible, the Saturday right before Easter. On this day, take your children to church or to the place where you attend church services on Sunday. If true to form, there will is little going on, because it is not Sunday when everyone shows up. As your children look at the inactivity and quietness of the church, explain that this does not mean a lot is not going on behind the scenes that they can't see. In fact, a great deal is probably going on, like the worship leader refining his or her music, a soloist practicing a few more times, the pastor making last minute changes to the sermon, Sunday School teachers reviewing their lessons, communion trays being set in place, bulletins folded, and contacts made to make sure everyone has a ride to church. Then, tell your children that so it was with Jesus, who continued to work behind the scenes between Good Friday and Resurrection Sunday, sharing the truth of who He was with those who had rejected Him. Finally, conclude with explaining that in the course of their lives, when they think God has forgotten them, He hasn't. In fact, God's silence means He is hard at work doing what is necessary to get them from the tough "Good Fridays" in their lives to the victorious "Resurrection Sundays."

As I conclude, I leave you with a poem a good friend of mine gave me not long before he died. His life was full of "Good Fridays" and *Silent Saturdays*; more so than most. Now his life is full of "Resurrection Sundays" as he walks everyday in the presence of God.

> Noontime darkness, who blocks the sun?
> His race has ended, our race begun.
> Anguished cry, the veil is rent,
> It is finished, His life's blood spent.
> Down it trickles, that precious flow,
> Giving life, to those below.
> Then cut down, a tomb to lay.
> Resting silent, for one more day.
> Bringing spices, that new day's done,
> They came to Him, but He has gone.
> Freeing us all, from Satan's prison,
> Hallelujah! He is risen!
> Reigning with God, His rightful place.
> Oh soon we'll see, His precious face.
> *Bob Gray*

The following verses referenced in this chapter can be found in sequence on my web site, www.tmoments.com. Click on the Book Resources button located on the home page.

Romans 3:23-25; John 3:16; Colossians 2:14; Mark 1:14-15; II Corinthians 4:7-12, 17-18; II Corinthians 5:2, 6-9; Luke 24:1-6; Mark 16:9; John 19:39; John 20: 6-9; Romans 14:11; Psalm 121: 1-3

TEACHABLE MOMENT 9
THE END IS EVEN BETTER
(Mother's Day)

Her children rise up and bless her...
(Proverbs 31:28)

Years ago, in the early part of the 20th Century, there was a wonderful novelist and short story writer named Irene Temple Bailey. Among the many subjects she wrote was a parable concerning a young mother. This parable, which has been cited on the internet, in many church bulletins, different magazines, and books, is the focus of this Mother's Day article. As I quote, rephrase, and draw from it, several Scriptures have been inserted to give biblical reference and further insight. As you read the revised parable, I pray this will help when doing the suggested Teachable Moment at the end.

There was once a young Christian mother, who like many others before and after, set her foot on God's sovereign path. As she did, this young mother asked the Lord if the path would be long?" God answered, "Sometimes it is, and often filled with many trials and tribulations. But at its conclusion the end is better than the beginning."

The young mother was happy in those beginning years and couldn't believe that anything could be better than the way it was. She played and swam with her children, gathering flowers with them along the way. As she did, the young mother often cried to herself, "Nothing will ever be lovelier than this time."

But sure enough the night came, and then the storms and the path grew dark. The children shook with fear and the cold, and the mother drew them close to her, and covered them with her coat of prayers. As they warmed themselves, they said, "Oh, Mother we are not afraid, for you have taught us that God is always near and no harm can really come to us."

The Lord is the one who goes ahead of you; He will be with you. He will not fail you or forsake you. Do not fear or be dismayed. (Deuteronomy 31:8)

The young mother said, "This is better than the brightest day, for I have surely taught my children how to pray and trust always in the Lord." Then, the morning came and there was a hill ahead, and the children climbed and grew weary, and the mother was weary, but at all times she said to the children, "Pray and put your faith in Him and you will get to the top."

For faith is the assurance of things hoped for, the conviction of things not seen. (Hebrews 11:1)

The children climbed, and when they reached the top, they said, "We could not have done it without you, Mother." And the mother, when she lay down that night looked at the stars and said, "This is a better day than the last, for my children have learned not only to pray but to have faith during their difficult climb."

The next day brought strange new skies which darkened the earth and clouds of disappointment took them by surprise. The children began to stumble in the storm, but the mother quickly said, "Look up, lift up your eyes to God who is your Light." The children looked and saw the glory of God, and it was so bright that they could see their way through the darkness.

In Him was life, and the life was the Light of men. The Light shines in the darkness... (John 1:4-5)

That night the mother said, "This is the best day of all, for I have shown my children God." The days went on, and the weeks and the months and the years, but as the mother grew older and weaker, her children grew taller and stronger, and continued to walk in the light of God's Spirit. *(Acts 7:55)*

Finally, the mother's days on earth grew more difficult and to a close. Her children were always there for her, even to the end. At last they all came to a hill, and beyond the hill they could see a shining road and a golden gate flung open. The mother said, "I have reached the end of my journey. And now I know that the end is better than the beginning, for my children can walk alone with God, and one day their children will do the same and follow in their footsteps."

The children said, "You will always walk with us, mother, even when you have gone through the gates." They stood and watched her as she went through them. And they said, "She will always be with us. A mother like ours is more than a memory; she is a living presence." [1]

But we do not want you to be uninformed, brethren, about those who are asleep (passed away); so that you will not grieve as do the rest who have no hope. For if we believe that Jesus died and rose again, even so God will bring with Him those who have fallen asleep in Jesus. (I Thessalonians 4:13-14)

Teachable Moment

In this Teachable Moment, take a walk with your family one evening after dark. Take a flashlight along with you. If possible let mom lead the way. After you have walked for a while, take turns leading with the flashlight. When you are ready to head for home, make sure each of the children have had a chance to be the leader. Sometime during the walk back, stop and put your hand over the flashlight. Point out to your kids how dark everything looks when the light is covered up. As your walk comes to an end, be sure to hang back a little, so your children can finish the trek home by themselves leading with the light.

Sit down and share with your family the following analogy. The flashlight is like the Spirit of God; He is always on and always with each of you. He will be with you even in the darkest of nights. The family walk was like the life journey each of you will have to complete during your lifetime. The darkness of the evening represents the darkness of this world with all of its temptations, false wisdom, and sin. Without the flashlight (that is, without the Lord), stumbling and losing your way in the world is inevitable. So, don't cover up the light God has given you through the Spirit, let Him shine. Praying and believing in God is the best way to keep the Spirit shining and showing you the way. Finally, letting your children lead the way home with the flashlight is likened to the day they will be on their own with the Lord, raising their own children like you did with them. As

Temple Bailey concluded in her parable, the end is even better than the beginning for you, at least from God's perspective it is.

For God, who said, "Light shall shine out of darkness," is the One who has shone in our hearts to give the Light of the knowledge of the glory of God in the face of Christ." (II Corinthians 4:6)

The following verses referenced in this chapter can be found in sequence on my web site, www.tmoments.com. Click on the Book Resources button located on the home page.

Acts 7:55

TEACHABLE MOMENT 10
PLAN B'S
(Father's Day)

"For I know the plans that I have for you," declares the Lord, "plans for welfare and not for calamity to give you a future and a hope."
(Jeremiah 29:11)

Encourage your family to do all they can to make Father's Day a special day. As a father, it always warmed my heart when my kids went out of their way to make me feel loved and appreciated on this day. I still have some of the cards they made for me when they were young.

Not all children are able to celebrate Father's Day the way they want. Some can't because they have lost their dads through death or family separation, and some can't because they were abandoned by their dads. In respect to those who have been abandoned, I share with you a story that brings an important truth about God and His alternate plans when things like this happen. It is a story that would be good to share as a Teachable Moment with your kids at the end of a Father's Day since it deals with a son and his father.

A number of years ago, when I was a youth pastor in the Bay area of California, I had the opportunity to minister to many young people from varying backgrounds. Not all of my high school students came from well-adjusted homes; some grew up in broken homes where the father had abandoned the family.

Ted was one of those high school students in my youth group who was abandoned by his father, and seemingly, couldn't get over it. His dad's desertion caused Ted to continually struggle, even though God supplied him with loving adoptive parents and many faithful friends in the youth group. For Ted, this alternative, God's "Plan B" so to speak, didn't work well for him, because he wanted his actual father to be his father in life. But that wasn't possible, only God's "Plan B" was, which meant Ted had to accept the Lord's provisions in regard to a father's love. Fortunately for Ted, as with all of us, God was very patient, understanding, and loving with him as he worked through his hurt.

Perhaps, the greatest example of a "Plan B" in the Bible was in the Garden

PLAN B'S

of Eden after Adam and Eve sinned against God. Before they did, they were under God's first perfect "Plan A", which was a life full of peace, joy, security, love, and every other positive description of which you can think. *(Genesis 2:8-10)* But after they sinned, their perfect life was over. Had God not stepped in with a "Plan B", they, along with the rest of mankind, would have perished right then and there. When God stepped in, His plan was very costly, for it demanded the sacrifice of Jesus the Son to pay for what Adam and Eve did, as well as the rest of mankind who inherited their sin. *(Romans 5:14-16)* Still, God's plan worked, because everyone who repented and believed found a bridge back to God. *(I Corinthians 6:20; Matthew 20:28; I Timothy 2:5-6)*

> *...If you confess with your mouth Jesus as Lord, and believe in your heart that God raised Him from the dead, you will be saved. (Romans 10:9)*

Ted had given his life to Christ but hadn't accepted God's "Plan B" concerning his father, that is, until a memorable youth trip. During this trip to Yosemite on a spring weekend, God spoke to Ted in an incredible way that completely changed his thinking about his dad and God.

On this trip, I took about 150 high school students from church to build better relationships between them as well as bolster their faith. In preparation for the Saturday morning devotion, I gathered them together for a time of worshipful singing near Yosemite falls. After we finished singing, I instructed each to find a separate place in the meadow to have a quiet devotion. Before they took off to do this, I asked them to read one of the Psalms and be prepared to share what they had learned from it when they returned. I also suggested that when they picked a particular Psalm, they choose one nearest their birthdays. For example, February 7th might end up being Psalm 2:7 or the 27th Psalm, because February was the second month of the year, and seven was the seventh day of that month.

After about forty-five minutes, the kids began making their way back to our gathering. The sharing was very rich as each student had a lot to say, but Ted's comments spoke the loudest that day. When he got up to speak, He said at first that he had no intention of reading any Psalm, because his heart was bitter about his dad that day. Although after a few minutes of sitting underneath a huge tree and looking up at the falls, curiosity got the best of him, and he began searching out the Psalm that matched his birthday. After he found and read it, he read it again and again with great intensity. After he finished reading it for the last time, Ted told us that tears began to well up within him, for, as far as he was concerned, God had spoken to him about his father. Of course, we all wanted to know what Psalm Ted read. After holding back for a minute or so, Ted told us it was Psalm 2:7, which read, *"I will surely tell of the decree of the Lord; He said to Me, You are my Son, today I have begotten You."* When reading those words, Ted said that he felt the Spirit of God within him saying, "You are my son Ted, and I am your father; I will never abandon you, no matter what."

As we listened to Ted talk some more, we could all see a growing calm come over his face and spirit as never before. This calm lasted throughout the weekend and long after returning home from Yosemite, because he had finally accepted God's "Plan B" in his life.

Lastly, in respect to Ted and that weekend, I would say this was the best Father's Day he ever had, only to be surpassed by the Father's Days his own children might give him in the future.

Teachable Moment

To help your children remember God's resolve to make alternate plans for us when life breaks down, take them to a nearby park where there is a creek, pond, or river running through it. Pick one, if possible, that has at least two ways to get across the water to the other side. If you don't have such a park near you, you will have to do some adjusting and pretending. When I lived in Boise, Idaho, several years ago, I had the perfect situation for this illustration, in that the main bridge crossing the Boise River was under construction. The only way to get across was to go down stream to an alternate bridge. Even though it was a little inconvenient, it got me across which was all that counted.

Regardless of how close you can come for this kind of set up, just make sure you have at least two ways or bridges to get across the water with your kids, one that is blocked and one that isn't. As you take the second, which is not blocked, draw two parallels with your kids in respect to what was taught in this article. The first is with Adam and Eve who lived a perfect life in the Garden until they sinned. When they did, it was like blowing up their bridge to God. But because God is unfathomable in His grace, He created a second bridge to Him by sacrificing Jesus the Son on the cross. Then emphasize to your children that in order to use this second bridge, repenting of sin and believing in Christ was the toll price necessary to get on the bridge.

In a second parallel, compare the first blocked or destroyed bridge to something you had hoped for in your own life, but didn't get. Then, take the alternate bridge or path you and your children took, and compare it to God always providing another way for you no matter what happens to the first. As He has done that for you, so He will do it for them.

Finally, for fun, have your children pick a Psalm close to their birthday. See if there might be a personal lesson in it for them from God. If not, then just end with Ted's story if you haven't read it to them already.

The following verses referenced in this chapter can be found in sequence on my web site, www.tmoments.com. Click on the Book Resources button located on the home page.

Genesis 2:8-10; Romans 5:14-16; I Corinthians 6:20; Matthew 20:28; I Timothy 2:5-6

TEACHABLE MOMENT 11
JOURNALING
(Helping your children remember what God has done)

Therefore write the things which you have seen and the things which are...
(Revelation 1:19)

When Paul the Apostle wrote to his fellow believers 2000 years ago, his words could be summarized as a journal of reflective prayers, beliefs, teachings, and practical faith experiences. Paul's Epistles, his journals, so to speak, make up about half of the books in the New Testament. Needless to say, all that Paul shared about his life has helped millions upon millions of Christians over the centuries. They helped Paul, too; they allowed him to go back and reflect over the faith experiences he had since becoming a Christian.

Your children may never write to other Christians about their Christian walk as Paul did, but one thing they can do is journal their own experiences in Christ as Paul did. And if they do, they will then have a written log for their entire life of all that God has done with and for them. Such a written account can help them in the years to come, particularly when their faith needs bolstering, for it will remind them as they read it again and again of how God worked throughout their lives.

I began journaling about my faith-walk when I was in seventh grade. I still have some of those journals today. It was a God-inspired undertaking, because no one back in 1962 was journaling about their faith experiences, at least, not that I knew of. Since that time, I have written dozens of faith journals which have helped me throughout my life to understand God's will and plan. As an example, the rereading of past journals constantly proves why God said "no" to me on different issues at different times. Even during my journal time the other day, I reviewed some requests I made of God in 1980. In recording my thoughts back then, I stated to the Lord how disappointed I was with His delays and silence. Yet, as I read it, I wanted to say, "No, Kent, you don't know what is ahead, just wait it out." In hindsight, as I read this journal entry from over 30 years ago, it calmed my spirit and strengthened my faith. As a result, I determined that if God was always working on my behalf back in 1980, He was certainly doing no less for me today.

Further, a faith journal is more than a diary, which usually only records daily thoughts, activities, and hopes. It is more than that as it includes your prayers, stand-out Bible verses, Scriptural teachings, the spiritual sayings you have run across, and the spiritual counsel received from others.

It is also an honest and transparent log listing both your victories and defeats in the Christian life. Therefore, within it should be the instances where you trusted God fully, as well as your own personal struggles with sin, faith, doubt, and frustration. It should mention those you love and respect and those whom God is working on you to love. If there is any comfort in writing the good and bad in your life then take note of David, who seldom hesitated to declare both in his.

In God, whose word I praise, in God I have put my trust; I shall not be afraid. What can mere man do to me? (Psalm 56:4)

When I kept silent about my sin, my body wasted away, through my groaning all day long. For day and night Your hand was heavy upon me; My vitality was drained away as with the fever heat of summer. I acknowledged my sin to You, and my iniquity I did not hide. (Psalm 32:3-4)

On a final note, in regard to the privacy of a journal, it is up to you or your children to share it with others, including those in the family. In my journaling, I have shared bits and pieces of my journal with the family and others but not all of it. As far as I am concerned, what I write is between God and me. I believe that should be so with your children if they journal. Neither my wife nor I ever read or demanded to read our children's journals.

Teachable Moment

If you are interested in building a faith journal with your children, there are some good resources to read before doing so. One of the best, in my opinion, is *"Journal Keeping, Writing for Spiritual Growth"* by Luann Budd. I like this book in particular because of Luann, herself, who is not only an outstanding Christian woman but an excellent thinker, speaker, and writer. She is someone I have known since she was 16 years old. I met her at one of my youth retreats when she dedicated her life to the Lord. She has faithfully served Him ever since. Her wisdom on journaling is well worth your read.

Aside from what Luann and other Christian writers have to say about journaling, I will share with you what I would do for this Teachable Moment. My seven suggestions come from what I have done in the past, as well as what I would have liked to have done.

1. Pick a small spiral notebook for your journal that is easy to handle. On the outside of the cover put a beginning date, and then later on, an ending date. Paste a picture on the front cover, one that stands out and is interesting. I usually pick old pictures of my family.

2. Title each journal with a theme that depicts what the year was about. You will have to wait until the year is over to do this, unless you are a prophet.

3. On the first page, list the spiritual goals you hope to attain during the next year or time period. On the last page, you will record the progress you made toward those spiritual goals.

4. Everyday that you write, post the date and a possible heading that reflects what made that day what it was. This will help locate something you might want to recall or rethink when rereading your journal later on.

5. As you begin to write, feel free to paste in other pictures or anything that is special to you, perhaps something nice that a person has written to or about you. Also include any helpful sayings, quotes, and Scriptures you study, or hit upon.

6. Write exactly what you are thinking or feeling, good, bad, or in-between. If you write a lot one day, don't feel as if you have to do the same the next.

7. Journal as consistently as possible. If you decide to do it once a week, then keep that appointment with yourself and God. I usually journal everyday now, but there were times in the past when I only wrote once every week or two.

On a final note, I leave you with some Scriptures you might want to include in your journal. They deal with many of the situations you and your children will face in the Christian life.

Temptation
And when He arrived at the place, He said to them, "Pray that you may not enter into temptation." (Luke 22:40)

Stress
And He withdrew from them about a stone's throw, and He knelt down and began to pray, saying, "Father, if Thou art willing, remove this cup from Me; yet not My will, but Thine be done." (Luke 22:41-42)

Concern for others
With all prayer and petition pray at all times in the Spirit, and with this in view, be on the alert with all perseverance and petition for all the saints. (Ephesians 6:18)

Courage
And pray on my behalf, that utterance may be given to me in the opening of my mouth, to make known with boldness the mystery of the Gospel. (Ephesians 6:19)

Discernment and wisdom
And this I pray, that your love may abound still more and more in real knowledge and all discernment, so that you may approve the things that are excellent, in order to be sincere and blameless until the day of Christ…(Philippians 1:9-10)

But if any of you lacks wisdom, let him ask of God, who gives to all men generously and without reproach, and it will be given to him. (James 1:5)

Hurts
Is anyone among you suffering? Let him pray. Is anyone among you sick? Let him call for the elders of the church, and let them pray over him, anointing him with oil in the name of the Lord…(James 5:13-14)

Thanks
In everything give thanks; for this is God's will for you in Christ Jesus. (I Thessalonians 5:18)

Forgiveness

Therefore, confess your sins to one another, and pray for one another, so that you may be healed. The effective prayer of a righteous man can accomplish much. (James 5:16)

Miracles

Elijah was a man with a nature like ours, and he prayed earnestly that it might not rain; and it did not rain on the earth for three years and six months. And he prayed again, and the sky poured rain, and the earth produced its fruit. (James 5:17-18)

There are no further Scriptures listed on the website in reference to this article.

TEACHABLE MOMENT 12
FILLING THE BUCKET
(Acts of kindness)

Be kind to one another, tender-hearted, forgiving each other, just as God in Christ also has forgiven you.
(Ephesians 4:32)

A little kindergartner exclaimed, "You're mean!". When I was a school administrator in Idaho, this is what I heard from a very frustrated five-year-old girl in one of my computer labs. Surprisingly, her frustration was not directed toward a schoolmate, friend, or even teacher, but instead toward an uncooperative computer. I laughed inside at the time and had to agree silently with this little kindergartner; the computer was indeed being very mean. It refused to help her and was way too conditional in its response. It simply sat there and refused to do anything until she did all the right things.

To say the least, that computer had no sense of kindness, for it made no effort to alleviate her stress. So, she sought help from another source, a kind and loving computer teacher, Mrs. McClain. Upon seeing this little girl's hand go up for help, Mrs. McClain (my wife) immediately made her way over to rescue her from her frustration. She changed a few commands on the stubborn computer, patted the little girl on the head, and said, "Your work looks wonderful." The little girl's face brightened and joyfully she moved on with her assignment.

Acts of kindness can never be overdone when raising children and can be accomplished in what you say and do for your children. Without consistent acts of parental kindness, children can quickly be emptied of the emotional and spiritual reservoir they need to survive in this world. A picture of a child without consistent parental acts of kindness is like an empty water bucket in the family garden. The bucket is intended to be filled so it can water the garden, and without the garden being watered, it will soon dry up and quit producing.

Likewise, without watering your children with regular acts of kindness, they, like the bucket in the garden, will only collect dust, dirt, and rancid rain water. The dust being feelings of being unloved; the dirt being the corrupted values of the world from which they may seek love and kindness, and the rancid rain being the unkind spirit they may develop toward others.

Acts of kindness (filling the bucket) permeate the Scriptures. They are noted in abundance from Genesis to Revelation. Jesus verbally forgave and affirmed Peter *(John 21:17)* even though he denied Him three times. *(Luke 22:59-62)* Essentially, He said, "Peter you are forgiven, you are forgiven, you are forgiven. Now go and fulfill the mission I have called you to. You have always been my disciple; you are my disciple; you will always be my disciple." *(Matthew 16:18, Matthew 28:19-20)*

Filling a child's bucket with encouraging words of forgiveness and affirmation is a critical part of parenting, but it must be blended with action. The old saying, *"Actions speak louder than words"* is true. It is one thing to say you love your son or daughter but another to act kindly toward them when they need it.

Jesus was the master of both word and deed. Aside from affirming words, He was a model of servant action. Without hesitation, for example, He humbly washed His own disciple's feet. *(John 13:5)* What an act of kindness that was! In another instance, when Peter angrily cut off a man's ear who tried to take Jesus to trial, He responded by lovingly reattaching it. *(Luke 22:51)* And He did this in the midst of one of the most trying moments of His life on earth. *(Matthew 26:51-52)*

Therefore, acts of kindness toward children must continuously be implemented in your parenting, that is, if you want them to be like Christ and survive the unkind world into which they have been born. Without such acts of kindness, they will likely begin to look like the old waterless bucket in the garden that has lost its purpose.

Teachable Moment

In this Teachable Moment, read over the different Scriptures cited above and focus on them with regard to kindness toward one another. Go and buy a bucket from the store that will hold a good quantity of water. Put it outside for awhile and let it collect dust, dirt, and possibly old sprinkler water. While you are waiting for the bucket to get dirty, begin making a list with your children of possible acts of kindness. Use I Corinthians 13 as your text. For example, what acts of kindness in this chapter would represent one who "bears all things, believes all things, endures all things, and hopes all things"? What kindness reflects one who is "not provoked, able to suffer long with others, doesn't brag, and isn't arrogant"? Then brainstorm with your children about the acts of kindness you have discovered from the

Scripture. Eventually clean the bucket up, and begin having each family member fill out slips of paper describing acts of kindness done to them by others in the family. At first, they won't fill the bucket, but keep adding to the bucket as acts of kindness are accomplished by each in your family through the months. When the bucket is full, or near so, take an evening with your children and empty it out to read some of the acts of kindness that were done. Afterward, put them all back, and keep adding to the bucket. Hopefully, one day you will have to replace the bucket with a barrel. What a thrill that would be, and what a home you would likely have!

The following verses referenced in this chapter can be found in sequence on my web site, www.tmoments.com. Click on the Book Resources button located on the home page.

John 21:17; Luke 22:59-62; Matthew 16:18; Matthew 28:19-20; John 13:5; Luke 22:51; Matthew 26:51-52

TEACHABLE MOMENT 13
TARES ON THE FREEWAY
(Why God allows evil)

Jesus presented another parable to them, saying, "The kingdom of heaven may be compared to a man who sowed good seed in his field. But while his men were sleeping, his enemy came and sowed tares among the wheat, and went away. But when the wheat sprouted and bore grain, then the tares became evident also. The slaves of the landowner came and said to him, 'Sir, did you not sow good seed in your field? How then does it have tares?' And he said to them, 'An enemy has done this! The slaves said to him, 'Do you want us, then, to go and gather them up?' But he said, No, for while you are gathering up the tares, you may uproot the wheat with them. Allow both to grow together until the harvest; and in the time of the harvest I will say to the reapers, first gather up the tares and bind them in bundles to burn them up; but gather the wheat into my barn."

(Matthew 13:24-30)

Several years ago after returning from a Bible conference in the Chicago area, I traveled in and out of two of the busiest airports in the world, O'Hare and L.A. International. Amazingly, both of these airports at the time were uncharacteristically calm; they were almost like ghost towns. Just days before was the 9/11 terrorist attack on America that knocked down the World Trade Center twin towers in New York City, destroyed many lives at the Pentagon, and killed a plane full of passengers over Pennsylvania.

As I walked through the quiet corridors, I thought to myself about the great contrast between the hearts of these terrorists and that of Christ 2000 years ago. These terrorists intentionally massacred innocent men, women, and children to attain for themselves a higher position in heaven, while Jesus, on the other hand, gave up His life to bring all who would believe to heaven.

For Christ also died for sins once for all, the just for the unjust, so that He might bring us to God...(I Peter 3:18)

For God so loved the world that He gave His only begotten Son, that whoever believes in Him shall not perish, but have eternal life. (John 3:16)

In respect to this tragedy, as well as other tragedies where innocent lives are lost, a few questions come to mind. Why does God let terrorists exist; or better yet, why does He let their plans succeed? Why does God ever allow anyone to hurt, abuse, or murder another? Why doesn't He just step in and protect the innocent when they are being attacked or victimized? Tough questions to answer, to say the least, but ones with which the Scripture can help. Additionally, as important as it is for you to know the Scripture in respect to God's allowance of evil, it's even more important that your children do. A great deal of their growing confidence in God throughout their lives will depend on their belief that God is always in control, no matter what happens, even when evil "apparently" wins out at times.

The Bible teaches a great deal about God's allowance of seemingly uncontested evil. From the very beginning, He has allowed evil to have its day through those who practice it on others. Israel was a perfect illustration of this when they were enslaved by the Egyptians for hundreds of years. The rulers of Egypt during this time, aside from afflicting Israel with harsh slave labor and daily beatings, also put to death their newborn sons. Later on in another dramatic demonstration of their evil, they were poised to kill all of the Israelites at the Red Sea. Had God not intervened and wiped them out, they would have killed hundreds of thousands of men, women, and children, because evil dominated their lives.

> *Then the king of Egypt spoke to the Hebrew midwives, one of whom was named Shiphrah and the other was named Puah; and he said, "When you are helping the Hebrew women to give birth and see them upon the birthstool, if it is a son, then you shall put him to death; but if it is a daughter, then she shall live." But the midwives feared God, and did not do as the king of Egypt had commanded them, but let the boys live. So God was good to the midwives, and the people multiplied, and became very mighty. Because the midwives feared God, He established households for them. (Exodus 1:15-17, 20-21)*

> *But Moses said to the people, "Do not fear! Stand by and see the salvation of the Lord which He will accomplish for you today; for the Egyptians whom you have seen today, you will never see them again forever. The Lord will fight for*

you while you keep silent." Thus the Lord saved Israel that day from the hand of the Egyptians, and Israel saw the Egyptians dead on the seashore. (Exodus 14:13-14, 30)

Your children may wonder why God allowed such evil to exist back then, and why He still does today. They may even question why God doesn't stop every act of evil. Is it because He can't keep up with all the evil acts people commit? Of course, the answer is, "No." God is infinitely greater than evil and its author Satan, as the Scripture teaches.

You are from God, little children, and have overcome them; because greater is He who is in you than he who is in the world.. (I John 4:4)

Your children may ask in response to a tragedy encountered in their lifetime, if God was angry with those whom He let perish. Once again. the answer is typically, "No," because as was true with the 9/11 tragedy, some who died were Christians.

The best overriding answer you can give your children to questions like these lies in a decision God made even before He created the angels and mankind. From the very beginning, it was never God's intention to make spiritual robots but rather, to make a creation that could choose Him or not.

God created man in His own image, in the image of God He created him; male and female He created them. (Genesis 1:27)

For I am the Lord your God. Consecrate yourselves therefore, and be holy, for I am holy. (Leviticus 11:44)

The choice to be like God or not began with the angels and continues on with mankind. Sadly, Satan, one of His highest angels, was the first to choose to reject Him. He opted for his own lordship instead of God's, and because of that, about one-third of the other angels followed. *(Isaiah 14:12-13; Revelation 12:4)* When God created mankind, beginning with Adam and Eve, they also were given the right to choose Him or themselves as the lord of their own lives. Unfortunately, they also made a choice similar to Satan's, the only difference being that they were honest and sorrowful about that horrible decision and presumably, sought God's forgiveness as shown by the way they trusted Him thereafter. He forgave them, but from then on, everyone born into the world was born with a sin nature that condemned them, unless they too were honest with God and sought His forgiveness. *(Genesis 2:16-17; Genesis 3:6; Genesis 3:15-16; I Corinthians 15:45; Genesis 4:1, 4; Genesis 5:1-2)*

The only reason God was able to offer this forgiveness to Adam and Eve, or anyone else for that matter, was because sin was taken care of when Jesus, the Son of God, came to earth to give up His life for it on the cross. When He did, mankind's sin was atoned, whether past, present, or future. All anyone needed to do then, and now, is repent and believe. Those who didn't through the ages, or won't today or in the future, will be shut out of God's kingdom, as Satan and his angelic realm were. *(Hebrew 12:1-2 Ephesians 2:8-9; Romans 5:8; John 3:18-19)*

The answer to the question of why God still allows evil and those who practice it to exist, has to do with the choice God gives to everyone born into this world to either believe or reject Him. Until everyone in each generation has the chance to make that decision, then the world will be filled with those who choose to reject God, along with the harm and evil they consequently bring on others.

Like the parable of the tares cited at the beginning, those bent on evil are not taken out because of their evil. Because of their continuing presence and the continuous influence of Satan, evil deeds of all kinds get practiced, whether it is abuse, exploitation, mistreatment, robbery, thievery, murder, or even mass murder as the terrorists did on 9/11.

Your children may want to know about those who innocently lose their lives because of others. What about those who have died in hurricanes, tornados, earthquakes, floods or tsunamis? Did they have a chance to choose God? In response, tell them the Bible teaches that God desires all men to be saved, and that His Son's sacrifice on the cross covers their sin when they believe. Let them know that God gives light to everyone, enough for each individual to make a decision to choose Him or reject Him before their lives end. *(II Corinthians 5:15, II Timothy. 3:3-4, John 1:1, 4, 9; Psalm 139:16)*

Finally, tell your children that God is always in control and that nothing ever catches Him by surprise. At the very moment those men, women, and children lost their lives in the 9/11 tragedy, God was already at work ushering those who had believed in Him into heaven. On top of that, He also turned their tragedy into triumph by using their sacrificial deaths to convince others to believe, since many realized that life can come to a quick end when evil is still in the world.

> *And we know that God causes all things to work together for good to those who love God, to those who are called according to His purpose. (Romans 8:28)*

Teachable Moment

In this Teachable Moment, take your children to a safe location where they can observe a busy street, highway, or freeway. As they watch the cars go by, have them pick out a few bad drivers. Ask them to describe why those drivers are so bad and dangerous. Probably, they will say something like the driver goes too fast, they weave in and out of traffic, or they don't really seem to care about the safety of others. Your children may even say that these drivers are only concerned about getting to where they want to go, no matter what that means to others. After making several of these observations, ask your children to predict an outcome for these drivers and the others driving around them. I believe they probably would tell you an accident of some sort might happen, perhaps even a horrible one that might hurt or take the life of another.

Then take their comments and make parallels to the tares, the people who do harm to others, and those who choose to be the lord of their own lives. At the same time, compare the others on the freeway to the innocent people who are sometimes victimized by those in the world who do selfish and evil things for their own benefit.

Then, draw a parallel between the freedom granted all the drivers you and your children see on the busy street, highway or freeway, to the freedom God gives everyone born into this world to choose or not to choose Him as Lord.

Finally, compare those who are the innocent victims in a car accident caused by a bad driver to those in the world who must suffer at the hands of those who are making evil choices. Don't forget to emphasize in this last parallel, that just as all the bad drivers on the freeway are not stopped or taken off the freeway, neither does God do that with those who reject Him and hurt others. Although, sometimes He does, just as a policeman does when he arrests someone and has their car towed away.

The following verses referenced in this chapter can be found in sequence on my web site, www.tmoments.com. Click on the Book Resources button located on the home page.

Isaiah 14:12-13; Revelation 12:4 Genesis 2:16-17; Genesis 3:6; Genesis 3:15-16; I Corinthians 15:45; Genesis 4:1, 4; Genesis 5:1-2; Hebrews 12:1-2; Ephesians 2:8-9; Romans 5:8; John 3:18-19; II Corinthians 5:15; II Timothy 3:3-4; John 1:1, 4, 9; Psalm 139:16

TEACHABLE MOMENT 14
HOLLY LOVE
(God's unconditional love)

...Love does not take into account a wrong suffered... Bears all things, believes all things, hopes all things, and endures all things. Love never fails...
(I Corinthians 13:5, 7, 8)

I want to share with you a Teachable Moment my family experienced a number of years ago that helped each of us better understand God's unconditional love. This kind of love is not easy to grasp in a world that is so conditional with its love. It's sad, but the world in which we live often says, "I will love you if you will love me; but if you don't, then I won't," or "If you quit loving me, I will quit loving you." This kind of conditional love is not the kind of love God has for us; neither is it the kind of love He wants us to have for others. In fact, He made a new commandment with His kind of love in mind.

A new commandment I give to you, that you love one another, even as I have loved you, that you also love one another. (John 13:34)

Before I go on to tell of this Teachable Moment, I am compelled to first mention the greatest unconditional loving act of all time–that being when God Himself gave up His only begotten Son, Jesus Christ, on the cross for us. He did this so that our sins could be forgiven and taken care of for all time. This event is recorded in the book of John, one of the most quoted passages in the New Testament. Sadly, one of the most ignored passages as well! I hope you haven't ignored it, because your life here on earth and throughout eternity depends on it!

For God so loved the world, that he gave his only begotten Son, that whosoever believeth on him should not perish, but have eternal life. For God sent not the Son into the world to judge the world; but that the world should be saved through Him. He that believeth on Him is not judged: he that believeth not hath been judged already, because he hath not believed on the name of the only begotten Son of God. (John 3:16-18)

This being said, let me get to the illustration that greatly improved my family's perspective on several aspects of God's unconditional love. When my son and daughter were elementary school age, they both wanted a pet very badly. Finally, one Christmas my wife, Myrna, and I relented and took the pet plunge. We bought a little dog we named Holly. She was a cute little Lhasa Apso with a wonderful temperament. Holly was a lot of work for us at first. Our two kids promised to help, but you can pretty well guess who took care of Holly most of the time, Myrna, of course. Regardless of how much time each of us put into taking care of this little dog, we all learned to genuinely love her. At the same time, we also gained a lot by having her as a part of our family, especially in regard to understanding the nature of unconditional love; the same kind of love God gave to each of us. For instance, everyday when we arrived home from school, she greeted us with incredible enthusiasm and joy as if we had been separated from her for years. The Scripture teaches that God has a similar attitude toward us each day.

> *Just as the Father has loved Me, I have also loved you; abide in My love. If you keep My commandments, you will abide in My love; just as I have kept My Father's commandments and abide in His love. These things I have spoken to you so that My joy may be in you, and that your joy may be made full. (John 15:9-11)*

Another illustration of unconditional love occurred when Holly would go against our wishes and cause us frustration, impatience, and even anger. When we would discipline her, no matter how punitive it was, she never held a grudge. Holly always forgave us and was quick to forget each reprimand. In a similar way, God also forgot our sins and forgave each of us in the McClain family. No matter what each of us had done over the years, or how many times we were wrong or selfish, God forgave us and put it in the past. Both the Old and New Testaments confirm this kind of love from God.

> *As far as the east is from the west, so far has He removed our shortcomings and sins from us. Just as a father has compassion on his children, so the Lord has compassion on those who respect Him. For the Lord knows our frame. (Psalm 103:12-14-rbk)*

> *The Lord declares, "I will forgive your iniquity, and your sin I will remember no more." (Jeremiah 31:34)*

Blessed are those whose lawless deeds have been forgiven, and whose sins have been covered. Blessed is the man whose sin the Lord will not take into account. (Roman 4:7-8)

A final example of the parallels between Holly's love and God's was demonstrated when we were all at home. Holly would follow us everywhere; all she wanted to do was be where we were. She did this because she loved us and liked being as close to us as possible. In a similar way, our family found that God was like this to each one of us. In fact God promised in His Word that He would never leave or forsake any of us; not ever! You know what? He has kept this promise as each of us can attest today.

For He Himself has said, "I will never desert you, nor will I ever forsake you." (Hebrews 13:5)

...and lo, I am with you always, even unto the end of the world. (Matthew 28:20)

Holly is gone now; she died a number of years ago. During her last days on earth she became very sick, listless, and incurable. My wife and I struggled over the decision to have her "put to sleep," but it was something we had to do for her sake. When we took her to the vet, neither Myrna nor I left her side until she breathed her last breath. Holly will always remain in our memories, but perhaps our greatest remembrance of her is how she unconditionally loved each one of us, just as God does.

Teachable Moment

In this Teachable Moment go through each of the passages of Scripture mentioned and quoted in this article. And if you have a pet, have your entire family spend a special evening with it. During this time ask your children to jot down what loving characteristics your pet exhibits, especially those that are like God's. Then find other Scriptures to support each characteristic if you can. If you don't have a pet, then go to a park where you can observe a dog and his owner, preferably one who has children with him or her. Then complete the assignment in the same way. Don't forget at the end to remind your children that the unconditional they have seen, is the same kind your family is going to try to have with each other.

There are no further Scriptures listed on the website in reference to this article.

TEACHABLE MOMENT 15
NARNIA

(Virtuous literature/ movies can help build your children's faith)

> *Finally, brethren, whatever is true, whatever is honorable, whatever is right, whatever is pure, whatever is lovely, whatever is of good repute, if there is any excellence and if anything worthy of praise, dwell on these things.*
> *(Philippians 4:8)*

Although there are many pieces of literature and movies in the theatres today that can be very destructive to your children's hearts and minds, there are some worth reading or seeing that can actually help build their faith. *The Chronicles of Narnia: The Lion, the Witch, and the Wardrobe* is one of those. When I saw it the first time with my grandchildren, I was quite excited and joyful when it was over because it was so wonderfully done.

C. S. Lewis was an accomplished scholar at Oxford University in London during the early to mid-part of the 20th Century. He was an atheist for many years before turning his life over to Christ in 1929. *(John 9:35-38)* He was led to the Lord by an associate and friend, J.R.R. Tolkien, the author of *The Lord of the Rings*.[1] Aside from the *Chronicles of Narnia,* Lewis wrote several other Christian books: *Mere Christianity* and *Screwtape Letters* are the most recognized.

Movie allegory

An allegory is the use of figurative language to explain a hidden meaning, often something spiritual or moral. I personally believe C.S. Lewis used the *Chronicles of Narnia* (a children's make believe story) to explain the forces of good and evil and the role of Christ and Satan in this world.

Figurative and allegorical language

I will not mention all of the figurative language in the movie, but only that which caught my eye, heart, and ear. If my interpretation is different than yours, that's okay, but in my efforts to explain this allegory, I went to Scripture as much as I could.

The main characters in the story were Aslan (Christ), the White Witch

(Satan), the animals (mankind), and the children (God's chosen leaders or disciples).

The main symbols in the story include the great stone (the cross), Aslan's death (the crucifixion), the breaking of the stone table (torn temple curtain), Aslan's miraculous recovery (the resurrection), and the final battle (the defeat of Satan).

Aslan

Aslan was a lion in this story which is an appropriate symbol to represent Christ. A lion is the king of the beasts as Christ is the king of us all. *(John 19:21; Revelation 19:16)* Christ is even called the lion of Judah in the book of Revelation. *(Revelation 5:3)* In this story Aslan was good, kind, powerful, and willing to give up his life for another, particularly Edmund, one of the children. The animals who served Aslan loved Him very much and were willing to fight for Aslan against the White Witch. Christ was also good, kind, and powerful. He loved those who were helpless, and was gentle with the afflicted. *(Matthew 8:2-3; Luke 7:12-14)* He was powerful too, enough so to stop a storm for the sake of His disciples, and yet, He forfeited that power by dying on the cross to save us all. *(Mark 4:38-39)*

The White Witch

The White Witch was an evil and wicked ruler; her reign over the animals who served her was through fear and oppression. Her kingdom was dark and depressing. She was very cunning, presenting herself as a beacon of light, which was a trap for the unaware. In the story Edmund fell into her trap; his foolish desire to be a king himself nearly caused his own death, which Aslan rectified by sacrificing His own life for him.

Satan is very much like the White Witch as Scripture proves, because like her, he rules through fear and oppression. His kingdom has always been very dark and depressing throughout history with all the people of this earth. Like the White Witch, he is also a great deceiver and liar as was proved from the very beginning with Adam and Eve. It is possible that Edmund was likened to Adam and Eve because of the temptation into which they fell with Satan. *(Genesis 3:4-5)*

The animals

The animals of Narnia talked, and some were combinations of half-man and half-animal in appearance. They either followed the White Witch or Aslan. Some of the animal-like creatures who followed the White Witch were more sinister looking, especially those doing her immediate handy work. The rest seemed rather normal. Whether sinister looking or not, it was clear that each of these animals who followed the White Witch was on her side as the final battle approached.

The animal-like creatures that followed Aslan were similar in appearance to those who followed the White Witch, except none of them looked sinister. The only other contrasts were that they seemed to be at peace with one another and loved their master rather than feared him.

The animals in the allegory are analogous to mankind. Just as each animal-like creature represented a different species in Narnia, so man is varied as well. Mankind today, as you know, is made up of many races, colors of skin, customs, and languages. However, as different as one man may be from another, all mankind is created in the image of God, by God. *(Genesis 9:6)* The only real important difference among men is whose side are they on, Christ's or Satan's? Like the animal-like creatures who aligned themselves with the White Witch, there are multitudes in the world that reject Christ as Lord and Master, and thus, have lined up with Satan. Some are more sinister and evil than others, but all are on his side. There are also millions who have accepted Christ as Lord and are on His side. The Scripture is very plain about these two sides. Jesus said it Himself, "You are either for me or against me." *(Matthew 12:30; John 3:16 & 18)*

Men, women, and children who have put their trust in Christ are like the animal-like creatures who served Aslan. *(John 1:12)* They are on His side because their faith in Christ assures them a place on God's side forever. *(John 10:28-30)* Some are definitively more committed than others. Like the animal-like creatures in Narnia, some chose to fight on the front lines, while others stayed near the back during the battles. In the end though, each will be rewarded according to the kind of fight they waged, but all will be in the kingdom. *(II Corinthians 5:10)*

The children

The children in this story were Peter, Susan, Edmund, and Lucy. They each had different roles, but all had one prophesied purpose, and that was to help Aslan save Narnia by defeating the wicked White Witch.

The disciples, as well as all of God's leaders throughout the centuries, are parallels to the four children in this story. From the very beginning of time, God has chosen and called certain leaders to help Him win over mankind and defeat evil.

The stone table

The stone table was the place where Aslan was taken to be slain by the White Witch. In a bargain to save Edmund's life, Aslan decided to offer his own life in exchange. The cross on which Jesus died is the parallel to the stone table upon which Aslan died. *(Colossians 2:13-14)* Just as Aslan freely gave up his life on a cold stone table for Edmund's, so did Christ give up His life on a rugged cross for all of mankind.

Aslan's death

When the White Witch tied Aslan up on the stone table, he was immediately mocked by all of her subjects, and his hair was sheered in a final act of humiliation. The White Witch then thrust a knife into his heart as everyone around the stone table celebrated. Christ's own crucifixion is the parallel to Aslan's. Just as Aslan was humiliated and slain on a cold stone table, so was Christ humiliated in his beatings and final death on the cross. *(Luke 24:20; Isaiah 53:3-5)*

The broken stone

The stone table, on which Aslan died, broke in two pieces shortly after the White Witch left to attack the rest of Aslan's forces. The torn curtain in the Temple at Christ's death is parallel to the broken stone table. The tearing of the Temple curtain signified the promise that there would no longer be a barrier between God and man. *(Matthew 27:50-53)* Christ's death on the cross assured us all of this promise.

Aslan's miraculous recovery

After a large earthquake and the breaking of the stone table, Aslan came to life, appearing to Susan and Lucy. The resurrection of Christ is the parallel to Aslan's miraculous recovery. Mary sitting outside the tomb of Jesus when He arose is parallel to Susan and Lucy staying by Aslan's side until his miraculous recovery. *(John 20:11 & 16)*

Final thoughts

C.S. Lewis' story about Narnia is a great allegory about good and evil, Christ and Satan, and man who is both saved and lost. The images he used to tell his story were clear and never confusing. This generation of children and young people today needs clear pictures of who God is and what He has done. They need to know the real authors of good and evil, whether it is abstractly taught or put in allegory form as C.S. Lewis did in the *Chronicles of Narnia*.

There are other children's stories about good and evil which have come out in recent years that do not present a clear picture of good and evil. *Harry Potter* films and books are a good example of this. Unlike the *Chronicles of Narnia*, the *Harry Potter* books and films confuse us about the author of good. Harry is a wizard for example, a figure in Scripture that is totally evil. *(II Chronicles 31:1, 2 6; Malachi 3:5; Leviticus 19:30-31; Deuteronomy 9:9-14)* To make a wizard a hero of good can only lead to confusion for this generation of children which desperately needs not only to understand what is good, but needs to know the real author of good, Jesus Christ. The argument is made that *Harry Potter* books are making avid readers out of children who found little interest in reading before. This may be true; the books are exciting to read. But, in the end, when these children grow up and have to face the great challenges of living in this world, it will not be their reading skills that will get them through life. Rather, it will be their relationship with the God who created them and with Christ who gave up His life for them, so they could have the abundant life they were meant to live. Embrace the *Chronicles of Narnia* and walk away from the *Harry Potter* books and movies or anything like them.

Teachable Moment

If you have already read *The Chronicles of Narnia: The Lion, the Witch, and the Wardrobe* or seen the movie, I recommend you read or watch it again with your children. Make comparisons to God's Word as you talk about the different characters and events in the story. Perhaps use some of the parallels I have mentioned along with the corresponding Scriptures. Focus on building strong beliefs within your children about what is good, which begins first of all with its author, the Lord Himself as depicted by Aslan in this story.

The following verses referenced in this chapter can be found in sequence on my web site, www.tmoments.com. Click on the Book Resources button located on the home page.

John 9:35-38; John 19:21 Revelation 19:16; Revelation 5:3; Matthew 8:2-3; Luke 7:12-14; Mark 4:38-39; Genesis 3:4-5; Genesis 9:6; Matthew 12:30; John 3:16 & 18; John 1: 12; John 10:28-30; II Corinthians 5:10; Colossians 2:13-14; Luke 24:20; Isaiah 53:3-5; Matthew 27:50-53; John 20:11 & 16 11; II Chronicles 31:1, 2, 6; Malachi 3:5; Leviticus 19:30-31; Deuteronomy 9: 9-14

TEACHABLE MOMENT 16
LAURA CROW
(Assurances in the Christian life)

O death, where is your victory? O death, where is your sting? But thanks be to God, who gives us the victory through our Lord Jesus Christ.
(I Corinthians 15:55, 57)

A number of years ago when I was a Christian school administrator in Idaho, I had the privilege of personally getting to know one of my faithful school moms, Laura Crow. She was one of the few moms who passed away during the time I was there. In the midst of her battle with cancer during the school year, she always cared for her children, hoped for the best, and protested very little about her terminal condition. The events surrounding Laura the year she died were a mixture of hope, discouragement, and a lot of ups and downs. One moment, it seemed like Laura might recover from her cancer, and the next, she was only promised a few short months to live. During these challenging times for her, many rallied to support Laura. Several school moms, staff, and friends regularly prayed for her, brought food to her family, drove her children to school, and gave wonderful words of encouragement.

In the spring of that year, a group of caring moms gathered together one afternoon in my office to conduct a healing service for her. We all laid hands on Laura and asked God to take the cancer from her body. *(Matthew 7:7-8)* It was a precious time; one we all have never forgotten.

For a while afterward, Laura seemed to improve, but not for long; her cancer worsened, and finally, she had to be hospitalized. Her pain grew unbearable, which moved some of us to begin to pray, "Please take her quickly, Lord." And God did just that; He took her to heaven only a few days after school ended.

The times we all had with Laura were unforgettable. I remember how funny and brave she was, all at the same time. Linda, one of her close friends, shared how one day Laura poured ice down her back during an important doctor's visit to which she had driven Laura. When Linda asked, "Why would you do such a thing during such a serious appointment?" Laura said, "So you won't ever forget this moment." On another occasion when Laura visited my office, I took a chance and cracked a joke about her cancer. Her response was as expected, she couldn't stop laughing. I told her the entire state of Idaho would never suffer an energy crisis as long as she hung around. All Idaho had to do was plug into her for its power needs, because of all the radiation stored in her body everyday.

I remember a conversation I had with Laura about Michelle, another mother at our school who succumbed to cancer. We were both at Michelle's funeral, and I said to her, "I'm so surprised to see you are here." Laura quickly responded, saying, "I simply wanted to see how Michelle's children respond to their mother's passing, and what it would be like from this end to be memorialized by friends and loved ones." As you can see, Laura was not short of courage.

Because of Laura's well-chronicled year with us, there were some biblical assurances *(The Father's Assurance, Gethsemane Assurance, Helper's Assurance, and Eden Assurance)* that helped answer some of the tough questions surrounding her difficult passing. Some of those questions were: why was it not God's will to heal her; what help was there for those left behind; and what enabled Laura to enter heaven?

The Father's Assurance
(Where is Laura now?)

There is a promise from Scripture that when believers die, they will immediately be in the presence of God the Father. This is the action the Father has taken with all departed believers throughout the ages, including Moses, Abraham, Laura, and eventually you and me. *(Matthew 17:1-3; Luke 23:39-43)*

> *But we do not want you to be uninformed, brethren, about those who are asleep, so that you will not grieve as do the rest who have no hope. For if we believe that Jesus died and rose again, even so God will bring with Him those who have fallen asleep in Jesus. (I Thessalonians 4:13-14)*

When Laura breathed her last, God the Father immediately swept her into heaven at that moment. What a change she must have experienced when this happened; one moment, paralyzed with pain and the next, liberated in the arms of God. She currently remains there with Him, along with other family members and friends who put their trust in Christ as Savior.

The funeral held in Laura's honor, which was not long after God swept her away, celebrated Laura's life. At the funeral, a coffin held her body, but Laura wasn't in it. In fact, by the time the first prayer was prayed, the first praise given, or the Word read at this service, Laura was already getting used to a new heavenly body and new direction for her life. *(I Corinthians 15:44, 40)* Her new body was a promise from God, and quite necessary to enable her to continue His plan for her life, which began all the way back when she was in her mother's womb. *(Psalm 139:13,16)*

The Gethsemane Assurance
(Why was it not God's will to heal her?)

Since the Lord decided not to extend Laura's life for which many of us prayed, what heavenly responsibility was required of her that overrode our request? In other words, what is Laura now doing in heaven that was more important than keeping her on earth with her family and friends? The answer is "we don't know," and really won't until we get to heaven to ask God, face to face.

> *For now we see in a mirror dimly, but then face to face; now I know in part, but then I will know fully just as I also have been fully known. (I Corinthians 13:12)*

Therefore, by faith we are to accept God's decision to move her to a superseding work, which is now in heaven. Simply put, God knows what He is doing, and one day, all of His decisions will make sense to all of us. (Romans 8:28) Who knows, perhaps the mothering Laura wanted to complete with her children on earth is better served by taking care of children in heaven who were lost to their parents.

In addition to the confidence we can put in God's sovereignty during a time of loss, the account at Gethsemane helps explain one of the major reasons why God often doesn't intervene, even when a miraculous healing is being sought.

> *They came to a place named Gethsemane; and He said to His disciples, "Sit here until I have prayed."...and He began to be very distressed and troubled. And He said to them, "My soul is deeply grieved to the point of death; remain here and keep watch." And He went a little beyond them, and fell to the ground and began to pray that if it were possible, the hour might pass Him by. And He was saying, "Abba! Father! All things are possible for You; remove this cup from*

Me; yet not what I will, but what You will." (Mark 14:32-36)

When Jesus entered the Garden of Gethsemane He faced an impending death. In response, He sought deliverance, but the Father said, "No," because a greater plan had been set in motion, one that would save mankind from its sin. In order for this plan to work, Jesus had to die on the cross so sin could be atoned. The Gethsemane application for Laura was pretty much the same in principle, in that God also had a greater plan in mind when taking her to heaven when He did. It is no different with any of His believers, including you and those in your family, when the time comes.

The Helper's Assurance
(What help is there for those left behind?)

When Jesus left His disciples to join the Father in heaven, He promised to leave them with the great "Helper," the Holy Spirit. God has never left any of His loved ones on earth to fend for themselves and this includes children who lose parents. When God creates a child, He makes provision for a completed job of parenting, whether here on earth or in heaven. (Philippians 1:6)

> *I will ask the Father, and He will give you another Helper, that He may be with you forever; that is the Spirit of truth, whom the world cannot receive, because it does not see Him or know Him, but you know Him because He abides with you and will be in you. I will not leave you as orphans; I will come to you. (John 14:16-18)*

During a job interview at a Los Angeles Orphan's Home in my college years, I was asked about my faith. The administrators who interviewed me wanted to know if I would share my religious convictions about Christ with the children with whom I would work. I decided to take a chance and answered them forthrightly, "Yes, I would do everything possible to bring these orphaned children to Christ." They quickly responded, "You're hired, these kids need Christ." As you might guess, these administrators were all Christians. Hence, I began working with these children as if they were my own, for all had lost their parents in one way or another. And, of course, my first priority was to help them develop a faith in Christ, as I did with my own children later on when I married and became a parent. As a result of the efforts I made, along with those who preceded and came after me, most of these children came to know the Lord, which helped them incredibly throughout their lives. I know because I was reunited with several of them during a reunion a few years ago; some were parents themselves. Needless to say, God did a sufficient work of parenting without the presence of their own natural parents. When God takes a mother like Laura Crow, He provides helpers in the wings for her children, just as He did with the Spirit when Jesus made His exit from earth.

The Eden Assurance
(What enabled Laura to enter heaven?)

The decision to let the Son die on the cross in order to restore all men to God was not really made at the Garden of Gethsemane, but in the Garden of Eden where Adam and Eve made their fateful decision to abandon God's lordship for their own. Wanting to be the lord of their own lives apart from Him was the "tree" of temptation they faced, of which God warned them not to partake. They did anyway, which infected the entire human race afterward with inherent sin. *(I Corinthians 15:22; Romans 5:14)* Although before this terrible choice began to make its impact, God initiated a plan to save and restore Adam and Eve, along with all those born throughout the ages who would put their faith in God, including Laura Crow.

The plan included eternal punishment for Satan and restoration for man through the compensating death of the Son. *(Revelation 20:10,15)* It was an incredible price for God to pay, because Jesus, the Son of God, would have to enter the human race, suffer terrible human pain, and endure humiliation on an ugly cross. His sacrifice, though, took care of sin and serves as a bridge for all who repent and believe.

Much like what Adam and Eve did, Laura expressed her regret for her own sin and believed. *(Romans 10:9; Mark 1:15)* This is why when she died, she was immediately swept into heaven, and why she will be there with God ready to greet her own believing children when their time is done on earth.

> *When the woman saw that the tree was good for food …she took from its fruit and ate; and she gave it to her husband, and he ate. Then the eyes of both of them were opened, and they knew that they were naked. They immediately heard the sound of the Lord, and hid themselves from His presence. The Lord responded, "Where are you?" Adam said, "I heard the sound of You in the*

garden, and I was afraid because I was naked; so I hid myself." And God said, "Who told you that you were naked? Have you eaten from the tree (I want to be the lord of my own life now) which I commanded you not to eat?" Because of this, the Lord said to Satan who was close by, from now on I will put a great breech between you and mankind (woman). You will one day be able to crucify My only begotten Son on a cross (a bruise to the heel), but His death and resurrection, will deal you a final, fatal blow (bruise to your head). After this, you and all those who have paid no attention to My Son's sacrifice on the cross will be cast into an inescapable hell, where you can battle each other forever. (Genesis 3:6-15-rbk)

Teachable Moment

To help remember some of the lessons learned through Laura's life and death on earth and in heaven, make a chocolate cake with your family. Make it like the life of Laura, with contrasting ingredients that are sweet, bland, or even quite bitter. For instance, the flour and shortening that make up a cake are rather bland, which for Laura were probably those moments when there wasn't any despair or lack of hope, the in-between times so to speak. The baking powder, vanilla, and baking soda are bitter to the taste when eaten by themselves. In Laura's life, they represent the cancer, radiation treatments, and final death she experienced. But also in the cake are sugar, icing, and chocolate which by themselves are sweet to the taste. These ingredients are like the love and care Laura received from, and gave to, her family, friends, and God during her struggle. The sweetness is also the assurances given to her from the Word, the Father's assurance, Gethsemane assurance, Helper's assurance, and Eden assurance.

After you finish making the chocolate cake, let it sit for awhile so your family can look at it as a finished product. Then, before cutting into it, remind your children that this beautiful cake you have made together consisted of ingredients that were bland, bitter, and sweet, just as life will be, even while trusting God and resting on His assurances.

The following verses referenced in this chapter can be found in sequence on my web site, www.tmoments.com. Click on the Book Resources button located on the home page.

Matthew 7:7-8; Matthew 17:1-3; Luke 23:39-43; I Corinthians 15:44, 40; Psalm 139:13, 16; Romans 8:28; Philippians 1:6; I Corinthians 15:22; Romans 5:14; Revelation 20: 10, 15 Romans 10: 9; Mark 1:15

TEACHABLE MOMENT 17
"NO," "NOT YET," "YES"

(Teaching children what to expect)

Ask, and it will be given to you; seek, and you will find; knock, and it will be opened to you, for everyone who asks receives, and he who seeks finds, and to him who knocks it will be opened.
(Matthew 7:7-8)

Teaching your children what to expect from God when they pray is one of the most important lessons you can share with them to develop their faith. It is because they, like you, expect God to listen and answer their prayers. But how many times in church have you seen some prayers answered, while others go unanswered. How many times have you heard, "The Lord really answered my prayers," or, "The Lord did not answer my prayers," or, "The Lord is taking an awful long time answering my prayers"? How many times have you said the same thing yourself? In regard to this, let me share three stories teeming with prayer requests, yet three different outcomes. At the end, which of these Christians had their prayers answered?

Steve Patterson

Several years ago a friend of mine, Steve Patterson, died of lung cancer; he was only 56 years old when he went to be with the Lord. Steve was quite an accomplished basketball player who played center for the UCLA Bruins during the era between Lew Alcindor (Kareem Abdul Jabbar) and Bill Walton. He was an integral part of a string of seven straight NCAA basketball championships. After UCLA, Steve played five years in the NBA and was head basketball coach at Arizona State University, chairman of Super Bowl XXX, and commissioner of the Continental Basketball Association. As accomplished as Steve was, his greatest attribute was his faith in God. I know beause I had some great conversations with him several years before he died and saw many good things he had done for the Lord. During those last days, he and his family prayed that the Lord would extend his life and if anyone was deserving of some extra years, Steve was that person. So, did

God answer his prayers?

Jacob Deshazer

In another story filled with prayer, an American World War II prisoner named Jacob Deshazer asked God many times to save him from the torture he had to endure during his imprisonment. Before being captured by the Japanese, Jacob was a crew member on a B17 bomber in the famous Doolittle raid over Japan. The Doolittle raid was comprised of several B17s that took off from a carrier in the Pacific to bomb Japan for the very first time since Pearl Harbor. It was deemed an impossible mission, since the bombers only had enough fuel to get to Japan and then to the Chinese coast, where they had to hope for the best. As a result, several men died, but Jacob survived his plane's crash and was captured. Over the next four years, he was incarcerated in one Japanese prison after the next, often being beaten and tortured to within an inch of his life. Even after giving His life to Christ in the middle of this experience, he was still ruthlessly mistreated to the end of the war when he was finally saved and released.[1] Did his prayers go unanswered when he asked?

Lillian Trasher

Lillian Trasher was a missionary, and her story is one of the most amazing you would ever want to read. During the course of her life, she impacted thousands upon thousands of children for Christ in an orphanage she founded in Egypt. She did this during the first part of the 20th Century when resources to do such a ministry were minimal at best. Because of all that Lillian did, she was respectfully known throughout the world as the "Nile Mother" of Egypt. From the very beginning of this ministry for God, every one of her prayers was answered in one way or another. This started by getting her to Egypt in the first place with little money and then sustaining her orphanage which housed hundreds of homeless children year after year to the end of her life.[2] In answer to the question, "Did God answer her prayers?" The answer is decidedly "Yes!"

Out of these three stories, was Lillian Trasher the only one who received answers to her prayers? The answer is a resounding, "No!" Both of the two men, Steve Patterson and Jacob Dehshazer, also received answers to their prayers. The answers were just not what they had hoped for at the time, but no less an answer from God.

The point is that **God always answers every prayer and does so immediately. This is a truth your children need to learn while they are young, because you don't want them believing that God didn't answer their prayers when actually He did.** God has three ways of answering prayer. He either says, "No," "Not yet," or "Yes." All three answers have their own reasoning and purpose in God's thinking and plans. Consequently, when someone at church says, "The Lord really answered my prayers", respond respectfully if you can, " Whose prayers hasn't He answered?"

No

When God says "No", He does so for a number of reasons. There are times when a "Yes" would turn out to do more harm than good. Jonah in the Old Testament is an example of when the Lord says, "No." Jonah wanted out of his responsibility to preach to the Ninevites. If God had said "Yes" to Jonah's want, then it would have been bad for the Ninevites who needed God, and bad for Jonah who needed to learn how to love the lost of this world. *(Jonah 1:1-3; Jonah 3:1-5)*

In another instance, sometimes a "No" from God is for the sake of others, as was the case with Stephen in the New Testament. Of course, Stephen's desire was to serve God for many years, but the Lord said, "No" and took him before his time. As He did, another young man named Paul watched from a close distance, which ended up contributing to his turn around toward Christ. Then later on God said, "No," to Paul too, particularly in respect to traveling and presenting the Gospel to many areas of the world he had not been to. Instead, God allowed him to be jailed and eventually executed. During his time in jail, Paul wrote many letters about how to live the Christian life. These letters became a part of the New Testament and have been read and studied by millions of Christians throughout the centuries.

Therefore, when God said, "No," to Steve Patterson's request to live longer, perhaps He felt Steve's death would cause some people to stop and reconsider their relationship with God, as happened with Stephen and Paul. *(Acts 7:54-60; Acts 22:3-4, 7-8, 20-21; Ephesians 3:1; II Timothy 4:5-8)* Regardless of the reason though, God answered Steve's prayer and took him to heaven where he was deemed more valuable in accomplishing God's work and will.

Not Yet

When God says, "Not yet," to your prayers, it's not a "No" from Him. It just means that before He says, "Yes,", a lot has to happen. This was the case with Moses, who wanted to free his fellow Israelites from their Egyptian bondage, but was not ready to do so until he had spent 40 years of delay in the desert with God. Neither were the Israelites ready to make such a courageous move to leave Egypt; it also took them 40 years to prepare their hearts. *(Exodus 2:9-14; Acts 7:30-34; Exodus 14:13-14)*

When God delays, many good things can happen. First, your communication with Him dramatically increases. This happens when over a long period of time, you pray, read His Word, listen to what He says through it, hear what He says through others who love Him, and then pray some more. As you do, God will begin to fill your heart with His heart, so that you will eventually know just what He wants you to do, and how to do it. Second, God desires greatly to talk with you on a daily basis, so that you can become as close to Him as He wants to be with you. To accomplish this He often creates delays and even periods of isolation. This was certainly the case with Jacob Deshazer, the Doolittle Raider, who became so close to God in his captivity that he readily forgave his captors, just as Jesus forgave those who put Him on the cross. *(Luke 23:34)* Then after his imprisonment, he dedicated his life to bringing the Gospel to all of the Japanese people, including those who tortured him. Due to this commitment, thousands upon thousands of Japanese received Christ, paving the way for many new churches in that part of the world to be established. This is what God-ordained delays can do, so don't feel abandoned or rejected if He should give you some "Not yets" in response to your prayers.

Yes

When God says, "Yes," to your prayers, everything is set from His perspective to do so. Nehemiah in the Old Testament, who often prayed for his fellow, persecuted Israelites, is an example of this. Because the time was right for God to restore them and Nehemiah's heart was right (in that he was ready to say "Yes" to anything God asked of him), an incredible undertaking took place. In restoring Israel, Jerusalem first needed to be a safe haven again for the Israelites, but it wasn't because all of its walls were either broken down or completely destroyed. Therefore God asked Nehemiah to rebuild them, and he did with God's help and wisdom.

However what was most amazing about this fete is that it didn't take a number of years to do so, only 52 days. There is not a construction company in the world today with all of its modern equipment that could rebuild the walls of Jerusalem in such a short time. But, Nehemiah did it, because God said, "Yes, it's time," and Nehemiah said, "Yes, I'm ready." You and your children need to do the same, so practice saying, "Yes," to God when He says, "Yes," to your prayers. *(Nehemiah 6:15-16)*

There are some important guidelines to be learned from Nehemiah's experience, particularly in respect to six conditions he met for God to say, "Yes." The first condition was there needed to be an immediate need. The lives of Jerusalem people were in peril without walls to protect them. *(Nehemiah 1:2-3)* The second condition was prayer, which Nehemiah did throughout the rebuilding of the walls. *(Nehemiah 1:4)* The third was repentance (asking forgiveness) to make sure everything is right with the Lord. In Nehemiah's case his repentance was for the nation Israel, whose sin had gotten them into their perilous circumstances. *(Nehemiah 1:6-7)* The fourth was Nehemiah's transparency; he never hid his feelings or thoughts from anyone as he proceeded to do God's will. *(Nehemiah 2:2-5)* The fifth was a commitment to do the physical work needed to get the job done, not just by Nehemiah himself, but by all of those in Jerusalem. *(Nehemiah 3:3)* And the sixth was a commitment to carry through no matter who or what obstacles stood in the way. *(Nehemiah 4:16; Nehemiah 6:16)*

All of these conditions that Nehemiah met also exemplified how Lillian Trasher prepared herself before asking God for anything. This was probably why she received one "Yes" after another from Him while establishing her Christian orphanage; one considered, even by today's standards, as one of the greatest ever built.

Teachable Moments

In this Teachable Moment, there are three memorable activities which will help you remember the three responses you and your children will receive from the Lord the rest of your lives.

The first is to purchase the life story of Lillian Trasher, by Janet and Geoff Benge. It is published by YWAM publications in Seattle, Washington. Read it as a family over the next few weeks or months. Comment on each answered prayer of Lillian's as you go. The second is to go over the six conditions for a "Yes" answered prayer, and then see if any in your family have experienced one or more of these before getting a "Yes" from the

Lord. A third and final activity involves two plates: one full of cookies and the other full of rocks. After you have shared the content of this Teachable Moment with your children, bring out the plate of cookies some frosted with a "No", some with a "Not yet", and some with "Yes" representing the different ways the Lord answers our prayers. But before you let them dive into it, replace it with the plate of rocks. Naturally, they will be surprised and will question why. They may even protest, but that's okay, let them do it. Then, switch the plate back to the cookies again, telling them as they eat, that God has always promised to give them what is good and never what is bad in response to their prayers. Sometimes His good comes from a "No" answer, sometimes it comes from "Not Yet," and sometimes from an immediate "Yes." But no matter what His answer is, whether "No," "Not Yet," or "Yes," it is always for the good, if not in the short run, then in the long run. Remember, He never, never, never, gives answers that amount to a plate of rocks. And He is never too early or late with His answer; He is always right on time with it.

> *Or what man is there among you who, when his son asks for a loaf, will give him a stone? Or if he asks for a fish, he will not give him a snake, will he? If you then, being evil, know how to give good gifts to your children, how much more will your Father who is in heaven give what is good to those who ask Him! (Matthew 7: 9-11)*

The following verses referenced in this chapter can be found in sequence on my web site, www.tmoments.com. Click on the Book Resources button located on the home page.

Jonah 1:1-3; Jonah 3: 1-5; Acts 7:54-60; Acts 22:3-4, 7-8, 20-21; Ephesians 3:1; II Timothy 4:5-8; Exodus 2: 9-14; Acts 7:30-34; Exodus 14:13-14; Luke 23:34; Nehemiah 6:15-16; Nehemiah 1:2-3; Nehemiah 1:4; Nehemiah 1:6-7; Nehemiah 2:2-5; Nehemiah 3:3; Nehemiah 4:16; Nehemiah 6:16

TEACHABLE MOMENT 18
12 CANS
(Faith)

I can do all things through Him who strengthens me.
(Philippians 4:13)

I recently read the story of Jonathan and Rosalind Goforth, two missionaries who demonstrated an incredible faith during their time on earth. In the course of their lives, there wasn't any concept of *I can't* in their thinking or vocabulary; only *"I can do this through Christ, who strengthens me."* Because of this kind of faith, they helped lead thousands to Christ in China at the turn of the 20th Century. Although they suffered the loss of several of their own children, were persecuted and beaten by the Chinese, and even abandoned somewhat by their church toward the end of their stay in China, they never quit relying on God's strength.[1] In addition to the Teachable Moment suggested below, I encourage you to read to your children stories like the Goforths because they can only strengthen their faith. YWAM (Youth with a Mission Ministries) published their story and other similar stories in a series titled, *Christian Heroes, Then, & Now*. These books can be located on the internet and are well worth the purchase.

Believing you can do anything with the Lord's strength as the Goforths did is essential to your children's faith, as well as your own. It doesn't matter what the challenges, issues, or questions are in life. If you trust that God will strengthen you when the time comes, you can believe whatever you need to believe, and do whatever you need to do.

In regards to my own life, this was particularly true when I first started sharing Christ with others. One of my first witnessing experiences was with Campus Crusade for Christ, founded by the late Bill Bright. This experience came in my junior year at college during Easter vacation.

Every spring in the 1960s during Easter break, Campus Crusade gathered together as many staff and Christian college students as possible to present the Gospel of Christ to students on break. In my area of the country, the beaches near Balboa Island in Southern

California were the target. During the day, Crusade sent hundreds of students to the beaches to share Christ and invite the students there to a nightly meeting at the Balboa Pavilion where the Gospel was presented. At these meetings, there were opening songs, performances by a Christian illusionist named Andre Cole, and some closing testimonies. An invitation was always given at the end to receive Christ to which many responded each night. Since Campus Crusade didn't have an official singing group of its own to open up the evening, they asked a group I was part of to come in and help. We were called the *Something Singers* under the direction of Sonny Salsbury, my youth director at church. There were about 25 of us who could sing, play the guitar, the drums, or even the ukulele, but none of us had much experience sharing the Gospel with others, at least not the way Campus Crusade did it. Regardless though, we loved helping them each evening and were very excited to see so many come to Christ.

For me, the week got even more exciting when some Campus Crusade staffers asked if I wanted to go with them during the day to invite college students on the beaches to the meeting. I remember saying to myself before saying yes, "I can do this; I can!" When I joined them the next morning at Newport Beach, I was shocked to see over 600 others there ready to pass out invitations and a booklet called *The Four Spiritual Laws*, which explained how to become a Christian. Even though there were so many of us, I was still a little apprehensive, saying again to myself and God, "I can do this, I can do this." Then, right before I started out with them, I was greatly relieved when Linus Morris, a Crusade staffer, came along side and paired me up with one of the more veteran Crusade members.

Then, all of a sudden, a bugle blew! That's right, a bugle! Someone actually blew a bugle, which started everyone off at the same time. You can imagine what the beach-goers must have thought when they heard that bugle and saw 600 of us headed their way. In my heart I thought this would never work, but it was exciting. The guy I was paired with exuded confidence in what we were doing. He was a young guy, like myself, but headed for Vietnam the next week. To this day, I don't know if he survived Vietnam, for I never heard from him again.

After we shared Christ with a few who didn't respond, we finally came upon three rather tough guys. In my heart, I was saying, "This isn't going to work; we can't do this." Nonetheless, my Crusade partner started in and presented the Gospel to them. After he was finished, he asked them if there was any reason they had for not taking Christ into their hearts? They each said, "No," so he led them in a prayer to receive Christ in front of everyone around them on the beach that day. He then got their addresses for follow up and gave them to me as we walked from the beach. He wanted me to write to each of the guys and send them some Crusade materials on how to develop their new walk in Christ, which I did.

As you might surmise, I learned a good deal about sharing my faith that day, as well as during the rest of the week at Balboa and Newport Beach. The greatest lesson, though, I learned in the midst of all of this was that if I trusted Christ and stepped forward with what I felt He wanted me to do or believe, then there was nothing I couldn't do. As the years passed and proved, this applied to every aspect of my life, including the need for extra strength, the basic provisions of life, freedom from fear, triumph over circumstances, happiness, release from worry, victory over sin, security, answers to loneliness, contentment, clarity over confusion, and confidence in God. All of which you and your entire family can experience also by just believing and saying, "I can do anything through Christ, anything!"

Teachable Moment

There are many *I CANS* to be claimed in God's Word. In this Teachable Moment I have included just 12 for you to go through with your children. Before you read this Teachable Moment to your children, send them out on a can hunt. Any can will do, but it would be best if they all were about the same size. When you have collected twelve cans, clean them up and take off the old labels. After the cans are ready, line them up and put new labels on them, as suggested below. Each can represents a part of the Christian life that says, "*Through faith in Christ, I can do this, or I can think and believe this way.*" As you do this, read and discuss with your children the self-assuring question attached to each can, along with the corresponding Scripture.

Now, this is a big assignment, so you might want to spread it out over two or three different sessions. Regardless of what you decide, find a place to put all 12 cans, perhaps in a reachable part of the garage. Tell your children that if they ever feel they can't do something, they should go to the row of cans. Let them know that they are free to take out and reread the questions and Scriptures. If they are too young, then remind them they can always come to you for help. Each time they go to a can, tell them to write down their name, the date, and why they chose that particular can. Then tell them to put all of that information in the can.

At the end of a few weeks, or even months, gather your family together again to look at the contents of each can. If there is one can with more in it than another, open it up first and talk about why that might be. Such may indicate a particular area in your family's life that God is bringing to your attention. If so, then take special note of this, and pray accordingly.

Can # 1
(I can have strength)

Question: Why do I say I can't do what is in front of me when the Bible says I can do all things through Christ who gives me the strength to do it?

I can do all things through Him who strengthens me. (Philippians 4:13)

Can # 2
(I can have the provisions I need)

Question: Why do I ever fret in regard to the provisions I need to live this life? Is not God always there for me in this regard?

And my God will supply all your needs according to His riches in glory in Christ Jesus. (Philippians 4:19)

Can # 3
(I can achieve freedom from fear)

Question: Why do I fear circumstances, when the Bible says God Himself will be with me always?

Even though I walk through the valley of the shadow of death, I will fear no evil, for you are with me. (Psalm 23:4)

Can # 4

(I can triumph over all circumstances)

Question: Why do I accept any measure of defeat when the Bible says that God always leads me in triumph?

But thanks be to God, who always leads us in triumph in Christ, and manifests through us the sweet aroma of the knowledge of Him in every place. (II Corinthians 2:14)

Can # 5
(I can experience happiness)

Question: Why do I feel unhappy when I can rejoice in the knowledge that God's loving presence is always within me?

Why am I in despair, oh my soul? And why have I become disturbed within? My hope is in God, for I shall praise Him for the help of His presence. (Psalm 142:5)

The Lord's loving kindnesses indeed never cease, for His compassions never fail. They are new every morning; great is His faithfulness. (Lamentations 3:22-23)

Can # 6
(I can be released from worry)

Question: Why do I worry when I can turn all my anxious circumstances over to Christ?

Therefore humble yourselves under the mighty hand of God, that He may exalt you at the proper time, casting all your anxiety on Him, because He cares for you. (1 Peter 5:6-7)

Be anxious for nothing, but in everything by prayer and supplication with thanksgiving let your requests be made known to God. And the peace of God, which surpasses all comprehension, will guard your hearts and your minds in Christ Jesus. (Philippians 4:6-7)

The steps of a man are established by the Lord, and He delights in his way.

When he falls, he will not be hurled headlong, because the Lord is the One who holds his hand. I have been young and now I am old, yet I have not seen the righteous forsaken or his descendants begging bread. (Psalm 37:23-25)

Can # 7
(I can claim victory over sin's bondage)

Question: Why am I ever under the bondage to sin again, with Christ in my heart and the permanent presence and work of the Spirit?

If Christ is in you, though the body is dead because of sin, yet the spirit is alive because of righteousness. But if the Spirit who raised Jesus from the dead dwells in you, He who raised Christ Jesus from the dead will also give life to your mortal bodies through His Spirit who dwells in you. (Romans 8:10-11)

Can # 8
(I can feel secure)

Question: Why do I feel condemned for my past, present, or future sins, when I have made Jesus my Lord?

Therefore there is now no condemnation for those who are in Christ Jesus (Romans 8:1)

I give eternal life to them, and they will never perish; and no one will snatch them out of My hand. (John 10:28)

Can # 9
(I can be liberated from loneliness)

Question: Why do I feel alone when I can call on my best friend, Jesus, who said He would always be there for me?

No longer do I call you slaves, for the slave does not know what his master is doing; but I have called you friends. (John 15:15)

...and lo, I am with you always, even to the end of the age. (Matthew 28:20)

...He Himself has said, "I will never desert you, nor will I ever forsake you." (Hebrews 13:5)

Can # 10
(I <u>can</u> find contentment)

Question: Why am I so dissatisfied with my present circumstances when I can by faith live a contented life in every circumstance?

Not that I speak from want, for I have learned to be content in whatever circumstances I am. I know how to get along with humble means, and I also know how to live in prosperity; in any and every circumstance I have learned the secret of being filled and going hungry, both of having abundance and suffering need. (Philippians 4:11-12)

Can # 11
(I <u>can</u> rid myself of confusion)

Question: Why do I dwell in confusion, when I can call on God to give me clarity and understanding in everything?

For God is not a God of confusion but of peace, as in all the churches of the saints (I Corinthians 14:33)

Ask, and it will be given to you; seek, and you will find; knock, and it will be opened to you. For everyone who asks receives, and he who seeks finds, and to him who knocks it will be opened. (Matthew 7: 7-8)

Can # 12
(I <u>can</u> trust God for the right results)

Question: Why am I so afraid to share Christ with others, when all it takes is faith?

Now faith is the assurance of things hoped for, the conviction of things not seen. (Hebrews 11: 1)

And without faith it is impossible to please Him, for he who comes to God must believe that He is and that He is a rewarder of those who seek Him. (Hebrews 11: 6)

There are no further Scriptures listed on the website in reference to this article.

TEACHABLE MOMENT 19
BE LIKE JOSEPH
(Persevering through anger)

He who is slow to anger is better than the mighty, and he who rules his spirit, than he who captures a city. The lot is cast into the lap, but its every decision is from the Lord.

(Proverbs 16:32-33)

Very few in Scripture had the kind of perseverance and control over anger that Joseph did of the Old Testament. Just think of what he had to go through in this respect, beginning when he was just a young man. Out of jealousy, his brothers sold him into slavery. As Joseph began working through that, he was falsely accused by his master's wife of sexual advances and was sent to prison for something he hadn't done. As he worked through his prison experience, he helped Pharaoh's cupbearer (poison taster), who had the opportunity to return the favor, but didn't at first. In the midst of all of these circumstances, Joseph still never let his anger take control of him, instead he persevered in trusting God.

Eventually, God stepped in and rescued Joseph, putting him in one of the most powerful and influential positions in the world. God could do this, because Joseph was a young man who trusted Him fully, no matter what situation came his way. He also was a young man who loved deeply and forgave easily. When there was an opportunity to take revenge, as was the case in paying his brothers back for what they did to him, he refused and embraced them as if nothing had ever happened.

This can be true for you too, whether parent or child, if you learn how to persevere through adverse circumstances and control your anger. As a result of Joseph's ability to do this, he ended up achieving far more than he ever dreamed and ended up a very happy man.

The following selected Scriptures summarize Joseph's experience, but reading the whole account from Genesis 37 to 50 would be even better for your family. Take a few evenings and read his entire story to your children; you won't be disappointed.

Now Israel loved Joseph more than all his sons, because he was the son of his old age; and he made him a varicolored tunic. His brothers saw that their father loved him more than all his brothers; and so they hated him and could not speak to him on friendly terms. (Genesis 37:3-4)

Judah said to his brothers, "What profit is it for us to kill our brother and cover up his blood? Come and let us sell him to the Ishmaelites and not lay our hands on him, for he is our brother, our own flesh." And his brothers listened to him. Then some Midianite traders passed by, so they pulled him up and lifted Joseph out of the pit, and sold him to the Ishmaelites for twenty shekels of silver. Thus they brought Joseph into Egypt. (Genesis 37:26-28)

Now Joseph had been taken down to Egypt; and Potiphar, an Egyptian officer of Pharaoh, the captain of the bodyguard, bought him from the Ishmaelites, who had taken him down there. The Lord was with Joseph, so he became a successful man. And he was in the house of his master, the Egyptian. It came about after these events that his master's wife looked with desire at Joseph, and she said, "Lie with me." But he refused… Now when his master heard the words of his wife …saying, "This is what your slave did to me," his anger burned. So Joseph's master took him and put him into the jail, But the Lord was with Joseph and extended kindness to him, and gave him favor in the sight of the chief jailer. The chief jailer committed to Joseph's charge all the prisoners who were in the jail; so that whatever was done there, he was responsible for it. (Genesis 39:1-2, 7-8, 19-22)

So the chief cupbearer told his dream to Joseph, and said to him, "In my dream, behold, there was a vine in front of me…" Then Joseph said to him, "This is the interpretation …only keep me in mind when it goes well with you, and please do me a kindness by mentioning me to Pharaoh…" Yet the chief cupbearer did not remember Joseph, but forgot him. (Genesis 40: 9, 12, 14, 23)

Now it happened at the end of two full years that Pharaoh had a dream, and behold, he was standing by the Nile. Then Pharaoh sent and called for Joseph, and they hurriedly brought him out of the dungeon… So Pharaoh spoke to Joseph, "In my dream, behold…" Now Joseph said to Pharaoh, "Pharaoh's dreams are one and the same; God has told to Pharaoh what He is about to do." So Pharaoh said to Joseph, "Since God has informed you of all this, there is no one so discerning and wise as you are. You shall be over my house, and according to your command all my people shall do homage; only in the throne I will be greater than you." So when all the land of Egypt was famished, the people cried out to Pharaoh for bread; and Pharaoh said to all the Egyptians, "Go to Joseph; whatever he says to you, you shall do." [Then] the people of all the earth came to Egypt to buy grain from Joseph, because the famine was severe in all the earth. (Genesis 41:1 14, 17, 40, 55, 57)

Then ten brothers of Joseph went down to buy grain from Egypt. Now Joseph was the ruler over the land; he was the one who sold to all the people of the land. And Joseph's brothers came and bowed down to him with their faces to the ground. (Genesis 42:3, 6)

Then Joseph could not control himself before all those who stood by him, and he cried, "Have everyone go out from me." So there was no man with him when Joseph made himself known to his brothers. He wept so loudly that the Egyptians heard it… Then Joseph said to his brothers, "I am Joseph! Is my father still alive?" But his brothers could not answer him, for they were dismayed at his presence. Then Joseph said to his brothers, "Please come closer to me." And they came closer, and he said, "I am your brother Joseph, whom you sold into Egypt." Now do not be grieved or angry with yourselves, because you sold me here, for God sent me before you to preserve life. (Genesis 45:1-5)

As for you, you meant evil against me, but God meant it for good in order to bring about this present result, to preserve many people alive. So therefore, do not be afraid; I will provide for you and your little ones. So he comforted them and spoke kindly to them. (Genesis 50:20-21)

Joseph's great secret, as you and your children will discover, rested with his choice to believe in God no matter what befell him. This equipped him to demonstrate the perseverance and control he needed to accomplish God's plan all along the way. Two of the best passages in the New Testament that reflect Joseph's dedication to God and the perseverance he demonstrated are in the books of Romans and Hebrews.

All things work together for good, to those who love God and are called according to His purpose. (Romans 8:28)

Therefore, since we have so great a cloud of witnesses surrounding us, let us also lay aside every encumbrance and the sin which so easily entangles us, and let us run with endurance the race that is set before us, fixing our eyes on Jesus, the author and perfecter of faith…(Hebrews 12:1-2)

Joseph lived out the Romans passage as he believed in the end that God would pull everything together, which He did. The race he ran was long and difficult, very much like a long distance run that seems to have no end in sight. Nevertheless, it does have an end to it, as was the case with Joseph and with great results, too! The same is no less true for you and your children; you just need to run it the way Joseph did, with perseverance and control over things that might anger you along the way.

Teachable Moment

Before giving the specifics of what to do in this Teachable Moment, let me describe a 26 mile marathon race I ran several years ago in Colorado. It was a grueling race that took months of preparation. As I ran the race, there were mileage signs of hope all along the way: 12 miles to go, 5 miles to go, and 1 mile to go. As long as my focus stayed on the path, I wasn't distracted by several temptations to quit. Eventually, the finish line came into view and the race was over. Afterward, the satisfaction of having finished such a long race was well worth the effort. In a similar way, Joseph must have felt relieved too when his race was over. Fortunately, He kept his eyes on the Lord the whole way, so that when the distraction of disloyal brothers, a foolish slave owner, or an undeserved confinement in jail came, he didn't flinch or slow his pace.

To remember a portion of what Joseph did, create a long distance race for your own family to run. Pick a distance that is a challenge, yet reasonable for all of you to finish. Before you begin the run, discuss with your children the distractions and obstacles that might keep them from completing the race. Then run the race and analyze how each of you did. For instance, what were the hardest parts of the race, or how did each of you feel when it was over? Then compare the race with the kind of race God wants you to run in this life, especially in respect to people who will anger, hurt, or disappoint you. Emphasize as you talk, Joseph's great resolve not to become bitter or revengeful, no matter what anyone did to him. And why was this? Because he refused to believe God wouldn't make it all right in the end. In his in-between time, until God made it right, he persevered by filling his time doing good for others, even good to those who had hurt him.

There are no further Scriptures listed on the website in reference to this article.

TEACHABLE MOMENT 20
TEARS ARE OKAY
(Teaching children how to comfort the grieving)

*The Lord is near to the brokenhearted and
saves those who are crushed in spirit.
(Psalm 34:18)*

Years ago when my son Brodie was 10 years old, he lost a friend and soccer teammate in a bike accident. It happened right after a soccer game on a beautiful Fourth of July weekend in Colorado where I pastored a church. My son's friend was tragically struck by a car while riding his bike. When Brodie attended his funeral, at first he didn't know what to say or how to act, for losing a friend was a new experience for him. He was very quiet during the entire funeral as were many of his other teammates. Only at the end when Brodie walked away from the graveside did he and the other boys burst into tears. I believe the boys attending finally realized what had happened to their teammate.

Many kind and wonderful words of sympathy were preached and shared that day, but I believe the spontaneous tears from the boys spoke the loudest to the stricken family. It was the comfort they needed most of all at that stage in their grief.

Jesus likewise modeled the same kind of response to those in His ministry who had lost loved ones. He demonstrated this most dramatically with Mary and Martha when they suddenly lost their brother Lazarus. Here are some Scriptural excerpts from that account.

Now a certain man was sick, Lazarus of Bethany, the village of Mary and her sister Martha. It was the Mary who anointed the Lord with ointment, and wiped His feet with her hair, whose brother Lazarus was sick. So the sisters sent word to Him, saying, "Lord, behold, he whom You love is sick". Now Jesus loved Martha and her sister and Lazarus. (John 11:3, 5)

*Martha therefore, when she heard that Jesus was coming, went to meet Him, but Mary stayed at the house. Martha then said to Jesus, "Lord, if You had been here, my brother would not have died." (John 11:20-21)
Therefore, when Mary came where Jesus was, she saw Him, and fell at His feet,*

saying to Him, "Lord, if You had been here, my brother would not have died. When Jesus therefore saw her weeping, and the Jews who came with her also weeping, He was deeply moved in spirit and was troubled, and said, "Where have you laid him?" They said to Him, "Lord, come and see" Jesus wept. (John 11:32-35)

So Jesus, again being deeply moved within, came to the tomb. Now it was a cave, and a stone was lying against it. Jesus said, "Remove the stone…" So they removed the stone. Then Jesus raised His eyes, and said, "Father, I thank You that You have heard Me." When He had said these things, He cried out with a loud voice, "Lazarus, come forth." The man who had died came forth, bound hand and foot with wrappings, and his face was wrapped around with a cloth… (John 11:38-44)

Even though Jesus knew full well that Lazarus would come back from the dead as He had promised earlier, grief still overtook him when he met with Mary and Martha. A deeper study of this John 11 passage actually describes Jesus' reaction to Lazarus's death as that of an overt shaking kind of grief. In other words, his grief was not just a tear rolling down his cheek, but much more. He also didn't hesitate to share His sorrow openly in front of others; He didn't hold back.

Of course Jesus could have responded differently, perhaps preaching a sermon on how all things work together for good for those who love God. This was certainly true, and might have been comforting depending on their states of mind. *(Romans 8:28)* He could also have told them to grieve for awhile, but then put their faith to work and move on with God's will. *(Philippians 3:13-14)* Jesus could have even challenged Mary and Martha to look at their loss more with joy rather than sadness, for Lazarus was in a better place with God the Father. *(James 1:2-3; I Thessalonians 4:14)* But Jesus chose none of these responses; instead He openly grieved with them. Encourage your children to do likewise when their friends have suffered a loss, and you do the same, too.

Teachable Moment

In this Teachable Moment the goal is to instruct and set an example for your children of how to respond to the tragedy of others. First of all, a quick answer that says, "Let's move on beyond this" is often not the best medicine for a hurting family even if such advice comes from a selected passage of Scripture. All Scripture is true and essential, there is no doubt about that, but not every passage is right for every situation.

Second, the pattern Jesus modeled with Mary and Martha is an example to follow to help others during a loss. To gain some experience, call your pastor and ask him if there is anyone sick, injured, or grieving who your family can visit. Before you go, gain some instruction from him and read the entire account of Jesus, Mary, Martha, and Lazarus in John 11:1-44. As you read it, note how sympathetic Jesus was with Mary and Martha. When you arrive at the person's house, have your entire family pray for those who are hurting. If tears come to any of you, let them come, but if they don't, then offer kind and comforting words. When you return home, talk about the experience you had together as a family. Discuss how you might follow up with those you have visited, perhaps writing them a sympathy card. Lastly, end in prayer asking God to give you even more experiences and wisdom to minister to those who are hurting. It might even some day lead them into the kingdom, now wouldn't that be wonderful for your children to experience?

The following verses referenced in this chapter can be found in sequence on my web site, www.tmoments.com. Click on the Book Resources button located on the home page.

Romans 8:28; Philippians 3:13-14; James 1:2-3; I Thessalonians 4:14

TEACHABLE MOMENT 21
THE MAN ON THE FLYING TRAPEZE

(Faith leading to salvation)

Now faith is the assurance of things hoped for, the conviction of things not seen. (Hebrews 11:1)

Years ago, while living in Denver, Colorado, my wife, Myrna, and I took our two young children to the circus. While in the big tent, which was the main arena, there was one act that caught us all by surprise. It was a man on the high-flying trapeze. At first, his feats seemed rather ordinary, because there was a safety net to protect him should he fall. We watched for a while but soon lost interest and began watching other ongoing circus acts. In our assessment, we each determined that with a safety net, who couldn't do what the trapeze artist was doing. Our boastful thoughts and interest quickly changed when a crew of men came and took the net away. Now one mistake probably meant an end to his life. Amazingly, as the man continued his act, he got more and more daring going from one death-defying stunt to the next. As the man's performance wound down, another man swung out from another platform to catch him in mid-air. As they locked arms, nothing could separate them. They both finished on the platform across the way, and rightly received a standing ovation. My kids couldn't believe what they had seen; they talked about it for weeks.

The man on the high-flying trapeze was a good biblical picture of man's lost condition and God's plan to rescue him. The platform on which the trapeze performer originally stood symbolized the beginning of life for us all, a life created in the image of God, yet one with a terrible sin nature.

God created man in His own image, in the image of God He created him; male and female He created them. (Genesis 1:27)

I will give thanks to You, for I am fearfully and wonderfully made...(Psalm 139:14)

For all have sinned, and come short of the glory of God. (Romans 3:23)

For since by a man came death, by a man also came the resurrection of the dead. For as in Adam all die, so also in Christ all will be made alive. (I Corinthians 15:21-22)

How did this sin nature come about? According to the Bible, it began in the Garden of Eden when Adam and Eve decided to reject God's command to not eat of the tree of good and evil. *(Genesis 2:15-17; Genesis 3:6)* By eating of the tree, they basically said to God, "We are in control of our own decisions and life, not you." In response, God tossed them out of the Garden to a life with heartache, struggle, and eventually physical death. *(Genesis 3:16-24)* Fortunately for Adam and Eve, this wasn't to be forever, because following their bad decision, they eventually made a great one, to respond to God with repentance and accept His forgiveness. We know this by the lives they later lived, which demonstrated worship and dependence on Him. *(Genesis 4:1, 3-4; I Corinthians 15:45)* Unfortunately for you and your children, and everyone else who has ever lived, a sin nature was attached at birth because of Adam and Eve. This is a nature which can be dealt with the way they did though, through admittance of wrong (repentance) and faith. Illustratively, such a decision is like the trapeze artist when he decided to make a leap into the arms of his partner to get across to the other platform. His beginning platform represented a life under the domination of sin, his partner being Christ, and the platform across the way, eternal life with God. *(Romans 5:18-19; John 15:15-16; Romans 6:5-7)*

Life on the beginning platform can be lived out in many different ways. For instance, there are those in the world who will live out their lives doing things that everyone would say were selfish, immoral, hurtful, or simply bad. On the other hand, there are those on the platform that live lives acceptable to most, but in reality their hearts are hardly different toward God than those obviously sinning. Because of this, they don't feel the need to get off the beginning platform; they just live out their lives consumed by their own brand of sins. Both of these, whether overtly bad or acceptably good, are like a trapeze artist who refuses to leap into the hands of the partner swinging out to grab him, and consequently, will never get to the platform where God stands.

Grabbing the hands of the partner who swings out seems like the only logical and right thing to do for the trapeze artist, after all, that is why he is up so high doing what he is doing in the first place. Is it not the same between you and God in regard to your salvation? Why are you here in this world, but to leap out and trust God for salvation? Granted, leaping out from a platform you have grown used to can be hard, even though God's platform looks to be so much better on the other side. His platform contains everything you need and more. To get there, though, you have got to let go of the old platform when Jesus swings over to grab you. When you do this, the Scripture calls it repentance and faith, the letting go of the old life dominated by sin for a new life in Christ.

> *Therefore if anyone is in Christ, he is a new creature; the old things passed away; behold, new things have come. (II Corinthians 5:17)*

Once you have made this repentance/faith leap, you will arrive on God's platform never to return, or even to be able to return to the old platform again. At times, you may act like your old self on God's platform, but God's Spirit immediately goes to work to clean you up. *(Romans 8:26)*

What happens if you fall while making your grab for Christ's hands or lose your grip while swinging across? Be assured, holding on never depends on you, it all on His strength, and He's got plenty of it. All you need do is put your hand out and jump, He'll take care of the rest. *If we are faithless, He remains faithful, for He cannot deny Himself. (II Timothy 2:13)*

> *I will lift up my eyes to the mountains; from where shall my help come? My help comes from the Lord, Who made heaven and earth. He will not allow your foot to slip. (Psalm 121:1-3)*

Teachable Moment

In this Teachable Moment, take your children to a park or school yard where there is high bar play equipment. Make sure the high bars are safe, not too high, and age appropriate. Then, show your children, if they don't know already, how to go from one bar to the next without letting their feet touch the ground. Explain that as they go from one bar to the next, they must let go of one bar to grab hold of the next. As they attempt to do this themselves, promise your kids that you will be underneath to catch them should they fall, like the safety net under the trapeze artist at the beginning of his act. After they have done this a few times, change things up a bit, and tell your children that on the next go around you will be holding onto their hands as they go from one bar to the next. And then climb up on top of the bar and do just that. They may not need you to do so, but do it anyway for the sake of relating this lesson on faith and salvation.

When you are finished doing all of this, sit down with your children and parallel the different parts they (and the trapeze artist) did with the teaching above. Ask them what the leap from one bar to the other meant, particularly in letting go of one bar to grab a hold of the other. Is this not what you do when you leave your old life dominated by sin for a new one dominated by God? When you held their hands during their leaps, doesn't this symbolize God's plan to save and keep them forever in His presence no matter what befalls them? Remind them that no matter how weak or what mistakes they may make throughout their lives, God is simply not going to let go.

My sheep hear My voice, and I know them, and they follow Me; and I give eternal life to them, and they will never perish; and no one will snatch them out of My hand. (John 10:27-28)

As you conclude your time, remember that as precious as your children are, they were born on their own platforms just like you, a platform in God's image, yet dominated by sin and separated from Him. Until they make their own decision to get off that platform and join God on His, they will grow up never really knowing Him. If they have already made that decision, then praise God with them for what they have chosen to do. And if they have not, continue to pray that one day they will; meanwhile, keep sharing your faith experience with them as the Lord leads. But don't force or push them, just let God do His work. He will!

The following verses referenced in this chapter can be found in sequence on my web site, www.tmoments.com. Click on the Book Resources button located on the home page.

Genesis 2:15-17; Genesis 3:6; Genesis 3:16-24; Genesis 4:1, 3-4; I Corinthians 15:45; Romans 5:18-19; John 15:15-16; Romans 6:5-7; Romans 8:26

TEACHABLE MOMENT 22
THE GHOST AND THE DARKNESS

(The influences of the flesh and Satan)

But I say, walk by the Spirit, and you will not carry out the desire of the flesh. For the flesh sets its desire against the Spirit, and the Spirit against the flesh; for these are in opposition to one another...
(Galatians 5:16-17)

Put on the full armor of God, so that you will be able to stand firm against the schemes of the devil.
(Ephesians 6:11)

When I went running the other day to get in shape for a long race, I was so tired at the end that I tripped over a well-marked curb in the street. The fall was really my fault, because I should have been walking instead of running that last mile. On other occasions, particularly within a race itself, I have been tripped by other runners, perhaps not wanting me to pass or beat them to the finish line.

In a similar way, there are two influences that will trip up your children's walk with God, as well as your own; one is the *flesh* and the other is the sway of Satan on the world surrounding you. Despite these two negative influences, God has given you and your children enough Scripture to deal with both of them, along with the overpowering presence of the Holy Spirit. (Romans 5:3-5)

In respect to this, what is the difference between falling down in your faith because of the *flesh* versus falling down because of what Satan throws at you? First, when you fall due to your *fleshly* desires and selfish decisions, it is often because you have relapsed back to the old sinful ways of doing things before becoming a Christian. Of course, your children won't have such a history of the old life due to their age, but you probably do, and they surely will if you don't teach them how to handle the sinful *flesh*. In respect to these *fleshly*-falls, each of them are your own fault; you can't blame them on Satan. Some Christians do this from time to time to escape taking responsibility for the sins they have committed, but they are wrong.

It wasn't Satan forcing them to do wrong, but their own choice to do so.

Reverting back to the *flesh* involves refusing to trust God for your circumstances and returning to the old life dominated by selfishness, self-satisfaction, and self-love. To no surprise, the *flesh* has a vast assortment of ways to carry out its selfish actions, and you are probably prone to one, two, or more of these. Impure thoughts, immoral decisions, selfish decisions, hero worship of others, lying, stealing, arrogance, bragging, jealousy, anger, revenge, and carrying on disputes with others are just a few the Scripture lists and discusses. *(Galatians 5:19-21; I Corinthians 13:4-6; Romans 1:26-31)*

Obviously, the *flesh* needs to be taken care of as quickly as possible, otherwise Satan will move in during these relapses to add to and do even further damage, just as a lion moves in on wounded prey when he smells blood. Here are some Scriptural guidelines to help get the *flesh* under control. I call these the four **R**s in *flesh* purging.

1. **R**epent of your sinful deeds before God and others. Identify what you know you've done wrong, and then ask God and those you have hurt to forgive you. And quit blaming Satan for every wrong you have done. *(Matthew 6:12)*

2. **R**enew your commitment to follow the Lord. Openly state before God and others your intention to do so. Ask faithful brothers and sisters in Christ to uphold you in prayer and keep you accountable. *(James 5:16)*

3. **R**eview the steps that led you to the *flesh*-fall and ask the Spirit to help you flee future temptations. *(I Corinthians. 6: 18)*

4. **R**eturn (mentally) your *flesh* to Christ's cross of crucifixion where the Spirit can continue to put it to death. This process is called sanctification, the gradual process of eliminating the power of sin in your lives. The process will continue to the end of your life here on earth. *(Romans 6:6; II Thessalonians 2:13)*

Just because a lot of your falling is probably due to the *flesh*, doesn't mean Satan isn't alive and actively tripping up your walk with God; he is! The difference in comparison to the *flesh*, though, is that Satan's primary focus is to get you to abandon your relationship with God. If he is able to do this, then your *flesh* takes over and does the rest of the damage to you and others. This was Satan's approach with Peter, Job, and even Jesus; all three were challenged to abandon their relationship or standing with God. *(Luke 22:31-32; Job 1:8-12; Matthew 4:8-11)*

The use of persecution, fear, temptation, and harassment were the primary tools Satan used to dissuade them from loving and serving God, and He still uses those same tools today with all believers. The reasons these tools of Satan have been so effective is because they bring with them the dread of being humiliated or killed by others for believing. However, unlike unsaved humanity, you and your children are spiritually equipped to handle these dreads and fears through the instruction and encouragement of the Scripture.

> *But we have this treasure in earthen vessels, so that the surpassing greatness of the power will be of God and not from ourselves; we are afflicted in every way, but not crushed; perplexed, but not despairing; persecuted, but not forsaken; struck down, but not destroyed; always carrying about in the body the dying of Jesus, so that the life of Jesus also may be manifested in our body. For we who live are constantly being delivered over to death for Jesus' sake, so that the life of Jesus also may be manifested in our mortal flesh. (II Corinthians 4:7-11)*

> *O death, where is your victory? O death, where is your sting? …but thanks be to God, who gives us the victory through our Lord Jesus Christ. (I Corinthians 15:55, 57)*

In addition to fear, Satan uses the hardships of this life: unexpected sickness, loss of work, financial reverses, and concocted lies, in his battle to damage your entire family's relationship with God. But even if he is successful for a time, be assured that God will step in and restore you just as He did Peter, Job, and others throughout the Bible. *(Job 42:10-12: John 21:15)* Incredible as it seems, God has the forethought to work a present or past defeat into a future victory, if you just trust Him. As bad as Peter must have felt when he denied Christ, he experienced great victory later on when God allowed him to preach the Gospel again to others. *(Acts 4:5-12)*

On a last note, your response to the attacks of Satan and the *flesh* are the same in one sense, faith in God is your strength to overcome both. Yet, there is also a different response to each. With the *flesh,* God usually will move you to flee from it; with an attack by Satan, He asks you to stand firm and not give any ground. In respect to this, here are two responses I suggest you use when tripped up by Satan's threats.

1. Don't flee Satan's threats, instead put on the full armor of God to do battle, as laid out in the book of Ephesians.

Stand firm therefore, having girded your loins with truth, and having put on the breastplate of righteousness, and having shod your feet with the preparation of the gospel of peace; in addition to all, taking up the shield of faith with which you will be able to extinguish all the flaming arrows of the evil one. And take the helmet of salvation, and the sword of the Spirit, which is the word of God. (Ephesians 6:14-17)

2. Use God's Word in every confrontation with those representing Satan's effort to sway you from your faith. Just the mere proclamation of Scripture often causes those to draw back who are serving his evil purposes. Jesus used the Word Himself when confronted by Satan in the desert. If He used it, you and your children should also!

And the tempter came and said to Him, "If You are the Son of God, command that these stones become bread." But He answered and said, "It is written, Man shall not live on bread alone, but on every word that proceeds out of the mouth of God." (Matthew 4:3-4)

3. When Satan causes you to be anxious about your past sins, which have been forgiven by God, remind him of his future and continue to resist. Then watch him flee. *(James 4:7)*

Teachable Moment

There was a movie produced a number of years ago called *The Ghost and the Darkness*. It was a true story of two lions in Africa who attacked scores of people in a small village. This was unusual as lions for the most part don't go after humans unless they are starved or cornered. The lions in this story were finally hunted down by two professional game hunters but not before over 100 villagers were killed. If the hunters had not succeeded in killing the lions, the entire village might have been wiped out. I actually visited the Field Museum in Chicago where these two stuffed lions were on display. They did not look too intimidating in their stuffed state.

This story in many ways is analogous to Satan's attack on both believers and non-believers today, for just as these lions attacked vulnerable villagers and hunters in the film, so Satan does likewise with all of mankind. Since the movie is violent, I suggest you show it to your children when they are older. Much of what is in it, particularly the viciousness of the lions, has some good parallels to help you remember who Satan is and what he is always trying to do to destroy your relationship with God.

If after previewing the movie, you decide to wait to show it to your children, I suggest a second alternative, which might be even better for remembering and visualizing what the *flesh* and Satan can do. The local zoo is what I have in mind, but before you go make sure it has a lion or other dangerous animals. Prior to your trip, read a little about lions, highlighting the fear and danger they bring to those in their environment.

After you have arrived and have seen some other animals first, make your way over to the lions cage or compound. Ask your children why such a strong cage is necessary for the lions. Of course, they will say to keep everyone safe from the lions. Parallel that to the bars of safety God has given to protect your children from the difficult circumstances Satan might throw at them one day to hurt their faith in God. The bars God provides for them are not made with steel, but their prayers, Bible reading, obedience to His Word, and faith. And then tell your children as they look at the lions again to note that they have pretty much resigned themselves to give up attacking others because of the bars. Because they are never really able to do so, a lethargy has developed allowing nothing more than an occasional roar. This is what you want for you and your children in regard to Satan, a powerful being who has grown lethargic toward you, because of the spiritual bars you always have in place.

Then switch directions and talk about the negative influence of the *flesh* in you and your children's lives. Create a story where a zoo owner had to leave for a few days, leaving the care of the animals to his staff. While he was gone, his young son decided to take over, and no one could argue because he was the owner's son. In doing so, the son made some terrible decisions and mistakes, leaving gates unlocked, repairing broken bars with duct tape, and not feeding the animals on schedule. As time wore on, many animals escaped, people were mauled, and the operation of the zoo became chaotic. Fortunately for the boy, he had the sense to call his dad, thus prompting him to return in time to put the zoo back in order. Now, draw a parallel between the young boy and you and your children when you take back control of your lives from God. When you do, all kinds of chaos breaks out, which not only affects you but others too. Instead of animals escaping and running wild, the chaos in your life results in lying, cheating, deceit, unloving attitudes, and cruelness which hurts others. Fortunately, all you need do is ask God to come back and take over, as the young son did with his dad. When you do, all is restored, something your children always need to remember when they ask for forgiveness, no matter how *fleshy* they were.

The following verses referenced in this chapter can be found in sequence on my web site, www.tmoments.com. Click on the Book Resources button located on the home page.

Romans 5:3-5; Galatians 5:19-21; I Corinthians 13:4-6; Romans 1:26-31; Matthew 6: 12; James 5:16; I Corinthians 6:18; Romans 6:6; II Thessalonians 2:13; Luke 22:31-32; Job 1:8-12; Matthew 4:8-11; Job 42:10-12; John 21:15; Acts 4:5-12; James 4:7

TEACHABLE MOMENT 23
GOD THE FATHER, SON, AND SPIRIT

(Explaining the Trinity)

Hear, O Israel! The Lord is our God, the Lord is one!
(Deuteronomy 6:4)

Before reading this article about God the Father, Son, and Spirit (Trinity) and then doing the suggested Teachable Moment, please note that this may take two, or even three, sessions to carry out with your family. Take your time for this may be the most important Teachable Moment of the 24 listed in this book.

When I was a young child, just beginning to understand the world around me, two of the continuous burning candles in my life were my grandparents, Mem and Pap, as I called them. I loved being around Mem and Pap because they were so loving. Never once did I question whether they would always be there for me; I just simply took it by faith they would, and they never disappointed me, not even when I entered the difficult adolescent years. They each played different roles in loving me. Pap was always the initiator and planner. On a vacation, Pap always planned it out, paid for it, and drove the whole way. Mem, on the other hand, made food, bought me new toys to take along, and constantly entertained me along the way. It has been many years now since they passed away, yet I still think about them often. It is their oneness of spirit in loving me and each other which stands out the most.

In a parallel way, Mem and Pap are a picture of what I believe God the Father, Son, and Spirit are to those who put their trust in Him. In relation to this, three aspects of God will be discussed: first, the different roles the Father, Son, and Spirit played in saving mankind; second, the love and respect they shared between one another; and lastly, their oneness as the Trinity, that is, being wholly God together and wholly God in each of their persons.

Different Roles

There are different roles God the Father, Son, and Spirit play in loving and saving mankind. The Father's role in the Trinity is more like that of a planner, setting the agenda and designating responsibilities for the two others. According to Scripture, it is He who sent both the Son and Spirit to earth to do what they did to win over mankind. In short, His role is very much like that of a good father today who loves and takes care of his family in the best possible way. This is perhaps one reason why the Bible calls Him God the Father throughout. *(John 16:28; John 17:18-19; John 5:26-27)*

> *Jesus spoke these things; and lifting up His eyes to heaven, He said, "Father, the hour has come; glorify Your Son, that the Son may glorify You even as You gave Him authority over all flesh, that to all whom You have given Him, He may give eternal life. This is eternal life that they may know You, the only true God, and Jesus Christ whom You have sent. I glorified You on the earth, having accomplished the work which You have given Me to do." (John 17:1-4)*

> *But when the fullness of the time came, God sent forth His Son, born of a woman, born under the Law. (Galatians 4:4)*

> *But the Helper, the Holy Spirit, whom the Father will send in My name, He will teach you all things, and bring to your remembrance all that I said to you. (John 14:26)*

In the role of the Son, Jesus' responsibility in winning over mankind was to teach them who God was, what He looked like, and how they were to respond to Him. After that, His most important role was to give His life up on the cross so that all who repented and believed could be saved. *(Luke 13:2-3; John 3:16)*

> *I have manifested Your name to the men whom You gave Me out of the world; they were Yours and You gave them to Me, and they have kept Your word. Now they have come to know that everything You have given Me is from You; for the words which You gave Me I have given to them; and they received them and truly understood that I came forth from You, and they believed that You sent Me. (John 17:6-8)*

GOD THE FATHER, SON, AND SPIRIT

And while being reviled, He did not revile in return; while suffering, He uttered no threats, but kept entrusting Himself to Him who judges righteously; and He Himself bore our sins in His body on the cross, so that we might die to sin and live to righteousness; for by His wounds you were healed. (I Peter 2:23-24)

The Spirit's role is to continually influence the thoughts, minds, hearts, and feelings of all believers who trust Him. In doing so, He empowers them to do what God puts on their minds to do. He reminds them of the truth they need to consider when making decisions. He convicts them of their sins, so they will abandon selfishness and wrong behaviors for a life filled with doing what is right. Unlike the Old Testament, everyone in the New Testament and beyond received the Spirit upon belief and got a permanent measure of His presence. Those in the Old Testament had all they needed to grow in their faith, but a permanent gift of the Spirit's presence, they didn't receive. There is likely more than one reason for this, but perhaps the most evident is that God simply expects more in reaching this world from the generations after Christ than before Him. Therefore, to help them a permanent gift of the Spirit was given. And as the old saying goes, he who is given much is expected to give much in return. *(Luke 12:48; I Samuel 11:6; I Samuel 19:20; Psalm 51:10-11)*

But you will receive power when the Holy Spirit has come upon you; and you shall be My witnesses both in Jerusalem, and in all Judea and Samaria, and even to the remotest part of the earth. (Acts 1:8)

But the Helper, the Holy Spirit, whom the Father will send in My name, He will teach you all things, and bring to your remembrance all that I said to you. (John 14:26)

But to each one is given the manifestation of the Spirit for the common good. (I Corinthians 12:7)

Finally, the Spirit's work today is very much like that of a loving mother, in that a lot of what He does is behind the scenes: building up, comforting, helping, and strengthening all who have put their trust in Christ. Like a mother who does all she can to teach her children how to do what is right, and avoid what is wrong, so does the Spirit in the life of every believer. He does this by comforting them when they are hurting and empowering them to be right with God in everything. *(I Peter 1:1-2; Romans 8:12-14;*

Ephesians 3:16; I Thessalonians 1:5)

So the church throughout all Judea and Galilee and Samaria enjoyed peace, being built up; and going on in the fear of the Lord and in the comfort of the Holy Spirit, it continued to increase. (Acts 9:31)

Love and Respect between the Father, Son, and Spirit

The relationship between God the Father, Son, and Spirit is remarkable to say the least. All three love and respect each other immensely. Even though each is God, and all three together are also God, they lead and serve each other without any measure of competition or rivalry. There has never even been the smallest hint in Scripture that either Jesus or the Spirit desires to take over the leadership role of the Father. Each is completely content to do what He does, even when that means humbly serving the other. And when it comes to receiving the glory for what they have done, without hesitation they hand it off to the other. *(John 15:26; John 15:1; John 16:13-14; John 17:24)*

The Father loves the Son and has given all things into His hand. (John 3:35)

Jesus spoke these things; and lifting up His eyes to heaven, He said, "Father, the hour has come; glorify Your Son, that the Son may glorify You." (John 17:1)

Now when all the people were baptized, Jesus was also baptized, and while He was praying, heaven was opened, and the Holy Spirit descended upon Him in bodily form like a dove, and a voice came out of heaven, "You are My beloved Son, in You I am well-pleased." (Luke 3:21-22)

The grace of the Lord Jesus Christ, and the love of God, and the fellowship of the Holy Spirit, be with you all. (II Corinthians 13:14)

The Oneness of the Trinity

Lastly, the unity, togetherness, and love demonstrated by the Father, Son, and Spirit, should be an example for all believers when relating to those in their own family. If they demonstrated this unity, then fathers, moms, and children alike would experience the full measure of all that God has planned for them while on earth. If all Christians were also to do the same with each other, then there would be far less friction and division in the church. What a message that would be to a world in desperate need of the Lord and all that He is.

> *The glory which You have given Me I have given to them, that they may be one, just as We are one; I in them and You in Me, that they may be perfected in unity, so that the world may know that You sent Me, and loved them, even as You have loved Me. (John 17:22-23)*

The Trinity is often the term used to describe God the Father, Son, and Spirit. It is not a word used in the Bible, but it is still the best description of God. The actual definition means three in one, not three separate gods working together, nor one god split up into three different parts.[1] Each of the members of the Trinity is wholly God, and the three together are also wholly God. There is nothing in this world like the Trinity, not anyone, nor any group. Therefore, you and I will have to wait until we get to heaven to fully grasp God being three and one at the same time. But this doesn't mean you can't have a very good partial understanding of the Trinity, which can be easily explained and translated to your children. The Scriptures help with this because they present God as one and in three persons from Genesis to Revelation. Here are a few conclusions that come from the Scriptures. First, the three persons of the Trinity are equal; none is greater than the other. It is only because of our sin nature that you and I try and put a value of one over the other because of their differing roles. For instance, the Spirit is no less greater than the Father because His work on earth is that of a helper, supporter, and comforter. Second, together the Trinity is one God, and has operated so from the very beginning when creating the entire world, including the angelic realm and mankind. The Scriptures bear this out. *(Genesis 11:7; Isaiah 6:8)*

> *In the beginning God created the heavens and the earth. Let us make man in our image, after Our likeness. (Genesis 1: 1, 26)*

The third and final point is that even though they have different roles, the Trinity is not three parts of one God, for each is wholly God within

Himself. If they were three different manifestations of one God, then they would never have talked with each other as they did. Nor would one have been doing one ministry, while another something completely different at the same time. Therefore, God is one, yet in three persons, not one greater than the other. *(John 1:3; Colossians 2:9; I Corinthians 8:6; I Peter 1:2; John 1:32-34; Matthew 26:39)*

> *Yet for us there is but one God, the Father, from whom are all things and we exist for Him; and one Lord, Jesus Christ, by whom are all things, and we exist through Him. (I Corinthians 8:6)*

> *There is one body and one Spirit, just as also you were called in one hope of your calling; one Lord, one faith, one baptism, one God and Father of all who is over all and through all and in all. (Ephesians 4:4-6)*

Teachable Moment

This Teachable Moment includes three activities, as one simply can't cover all that God the Father, Son, and Spirit are. The first one is a candle that illustrates the different roles of the Father, Son, and Spirit. The second includes a family that demonstrates love and respect for each other while carrying out a mission of outreach. The third deals with what the Trinity is and is not.

A candle

In this illustration, have your children set up an unlit candle in a room that is dark. The darkness represents the world without God. Then, ask your children to light the candle. While they are doing this, tell them about God in three persons and what He does to win mankind back to Him.

When the wick is lit, identify the candle as Christ who comes into the world to show clearly what God looks like and is in every way. Tell your children, that the light of Christ will never fade for those who believe in Him. It is like a candle that can never burn out.

Then, ask your children to put their fingers near the candle, but not too close as you don't want them to burn themselves. Tell them that the heat they feel is like the ministry of the Holy Spirit, in that they can't see Him, but can always feel His presence.

Compare the Father to the match that lit the candle, and the oxygen that allowed it to stay lit. His role is somewhat the same for He is the One amongst the Trinity who sets things in motion and keeps them going from His position in heaven.

A loving family

In this illustration, sit down with your family and pick a project to do together that will help someone else, particularly a person in need. Perhaps, this might be someone in your church who is very lonely or without a family. Invite them over for dinner one evening, but as you prepare, give each in your family something to do to make this happen. Possibly, one can issue the invitation, while others help prepare the food, setting the table, or clean up afterward. Other things can also be done like buying a gift or card for the guest or guests, giving kind and assuring words during the meal, and praying for them before and after they have left.

After you are done, meet together and give respect and love to each in your family for what they did. Then, compare this to the respect and love God the Father, Son, and Spirit continuously give each other. Remind your children, that just as the Trinity never put one of themselves and what they did over the other, neither should they with their brothers or sisters.

An apple

Use this illustration to explain what the Trinity is and is not. Take an apple and have your children cut it into three equal parts (if they are old enough to do so without cutting themselves). Tell them this is not a picture of who God is; He is not a God divided into three parts. Then, cut another apple with each slice a little bigger than the other. Tell your children this is also not who God is, for the Father, Son, and Spirit are equal in all ways. Finally, take three apples, and put them side by side in a cellophane bag, and title the bag "apple," not "apples," but "apple." Teach your children that this is most likely what God is, three whole apples by themselves, side-by-side in a bag titled apple; God is both three and one at the same time.

The following verses referenced in this chapter can be found in sequence on my web site, www.tmoments.com. Click on the Book Resources button located on the home page.

John 16:28; John 17:18-19; John 5:26-27; Luke 13:2-3; John 3:16; Luke 12:48; I Samuel 11:6; I Samuel 19:20; Psalm 51:10-11; I Peter 1:1-2; Romans 8:12-14; Ephesians 3:16; I Thessalonians 1:5; John 15:26; John 15:1; John 16:13-14; John 17: 24; Genesis 11:7; Isaiah 6:8; John 1:3; Colossians 2:9; I Corinthians 8:6; I Peter 1:2; John 1:32-34; Matthew 26:39

TEACHABLE MOMENT 24
A BREAK IN THE DAM
(The Spirit's entrance after salvation)

He who believes in Me, as the Scripture said, "From his innermost being will flow rivers of living water." But this He spoke of the Spirit, whom those who believed in Him were to receive…
(John 7:38-39)

Several years ago, I read of a little toddler who mistakenly crawled out the back door of her home. At the outset, this didn't seem so alarming, except for the weather conditions; the temperatures were well below freezing. Evidently, without her mother's awareness, the little girl made her way into the backyard where she actually froze in her tracks. When the mother discovered her, paramedics were immediately called. For over an hour they tried to revive the little girl, seemingly without hope. Then, all of a sudden, a pulse was felt, her heart began beating, and life returned to her little body. Because of some very determined rescuers and the grace of God, she survived a very close call with death. For the mother the outcome was wonderful, as you can imagine. I'm sure she never forgot what could have happened had her daughter's spirit not been revived and brought to life. In a parallel way, when you and your children received Christ, God spiritually brought you to life; He gave you His Spirit, the Holy Spirit, to keep you safe and secure in His presence forever. *(I Peter 3:18; I John 4:13)*

> *When you were dead in your transgressions…He made you alive together with Him, having forgiven us all our transgressions. (Colossians 2:13)*

> *…and I give eternal life to them, and they will never perish; and no one will snatch them out of My hand. (John 10:28)*

Some say it takes a second dramatic decision or response to receive the Spirit. This is not the case, as Jesus said that if you believe, then you will receive the Spirit.

I will ask the Father, and He will give you another Helper, that He may be with you forever; that is the Spirit of truth, whom the world cannot receive, because it does not see Him or know Him, but you know Him because He abides with you and will be in you. But the Helper, the Holy Spirit, whom the Father will send in My name, He will teach you all things, and bring to your remembrance all that I said to you. (John 14:16-17, 26)

When receiving the Spirit upon belief, there are a variety of ways to respond, depending upon your personality or the set of circumstances that led you to Christ. If you are more outward going in your personality, you may respond dramatically when receiving Christ and the Holy Spirit. If on the other hand, you are quiet in spirit by nature, you will probably respond accordingly, but no less fulfilled or full of the Holy Spirit. If you have had a hard life before receiving Christ, then you may react more demonstratively because of the incredible changes the Lord immediately brought to your life. Paul and some of the other disciples were examples of these varied responses. Paul was more demonstrative because God turned his blindness into sight upon belief. Andrew, James, and John were less so, along with multitudes of other Christians throughout the centuries. *(Acts 9:17-21, Matthew 4:18-20)*

During the first few years after Christ's death and resurrection, many believers received the Spirit in a second and seemingly separate, event. Sometimes this was accompanied by the gift of tongues and sometimes not. This was necessary because many of them had accepted Christ while He was still on earth before His death and resurrection. During this time, the Spirit had a different ministry in the lives of believers, which included moving in and out of their hearts to accomplish God's overall will and purpose. When Jesus made His exit, the Spirit's ministry changed to a permanent filling upon belief. To dramatize this change, the Spirit miraculously entered several groups of Christians during those first days of the church. *(Acts 2:2-4)*

Needless to say, over the centuries there has been too much argument between Christians over the indwelling of the Spirit. Regardless of this, there are other indisputable truths about the Spirit all of us should rally around, one being that no matter how young or old you are when receiving Christ, you get just as much of the Spirit as all other believers do.

This means that your own children, no matter their age, have received just as much of the Holy Spirit as you have. This being true, then the goal for each of you and your children is to let the Spirit do His work in the decisions you make, no matter how adult-or child-based they are. *(I Corinthians 12:7, 13; Ephesians 4:4-6)*

Perhaps **the most important point concerning the ministry of the Spirit is that whatever decisions you or your children make, the Spirit will never leave you.** This even includes decisions that lead to bad, sinful, and even rebellious behavior. And when you finally decide to make things right, as the indwelling Spirit will always be pushing you to do, He will immediately help you recover, like those who rescued that little girl frozen in the snow.

Finally, the struggle remains: How can you tell if you are walking according to the Spirit or according to your own will and strength? A Christian who lives a life without letting the Spirit stay in control, lives one analogous to the little girl frozen in her footsteps: spiritually cold, motionless, and almost lifeless. In respect to your children, such a life can be dominated by one, two, or several behaviors; such as cheating, lying, making fun of others, and demanding their own way. It can also include being jealous, deceitful, angry, and disobedient to the rules set in your home and at school. For you, such a life without the control of the Spirit may include some of these same behaviors, along with many more adult-like sins which can get rather extreme as the Scripture describes. *(Galatians 5:19-21; Luke 11:39-42)*

In addition to what the Scriptures teach about not being under the Spirit's control, they also teach how to get back on track with Him. And when you do, those cold, motionless, and lifeless behaviors that were dominating your life will stop. The Spirit's restoration begins with being sorry for your actions, and ends with asking Him to take back the control of your life. It's that simple; the Spirit responds quickly to your confession and desire to have Him back in control. In some cases, He even regains control before you say a word, because He sees your heart and where it's going. Here are a few passages to help you get Him back in control.

> *Be gracious to me, oh God, according to Your lovingkindness; according to the greatness of Your compassion blot out my transgressions. Wash me thoroughly from my iniquity and cleanse me from my sin. For I know my transgressions...* *(Psalm 51:1-3)*

> *Be anxious for nothing, but in everything by prayer and supplication with thanksgiving let your requests be made known to God. (Ephesians 4:6)*

> *And all things you ask in prayer, believing, you will receive. (Matthew 21:22)*

That He would grant you...to be strengthened with power through His Spirit in the inner man. (Ephesians 3:16)

After you have made things right, the Spirit then picks up where He left off when you stopped trusting. He begins by flooding every area of your life with love, joy, peace, patience, goodness, kindness, and so many other similar qualities described in the Word. *(Galatians 5:22-23)* In a sense, what the Spirit does is analogous to a dam breaking and flooding everything below it. Except in your case, the dam represents your resistance to let the Spirit do His work. The breaking of the dam thus symbolizes your decision to let Him flood your life once again with His righteousness. The shorelines, coves, and inlets below the dam stand for all the areas in your life that need a full measure of His presence and strength. *(Romans 5:5)*

Teachable Moment

In this Teachable Moment, create a structure in the likeness of a dam with your children. This can be accomplished in the family bathtub, the backyard, or beach nearby.

As you build this little dam, picture for your children the valley below it where some beautiful trees, flowers, plants are growing. Then point out that because the dam was built, all of the lush foliage below it will struggle to survive, since the water it needs, will be shut off. Explain that if the dam isn't broken in one way or another and the water released, then the foliage will eventually shrivel up.

Before you have your children break the dam to give relief to what's pictured below, teach them about the ministry of the Spirit in their lives. Use the teaching and Scriptures above to help. Be sure while doing this to draw a comparison between their refusal to let the Spirit be in control of their own lives to the construction of the dam which keeps water from the foliage below. Explain to them how letting the water through their dam parallels letting the Spirit flow freely once again into their lives. Then, draw an analogy between the shorelines, coves, and inlets you have pictured to the different areas in you and your children's lives that need the flow of the Spirit. Identify what those areas are in your lives, and what you see the Spirit doing with them.

When you have finished with this part of the Teachable Moment, take the illustration of the dam a point further. Rebuild the dam again and again, one for each member of your family. This will give all of you the opportunity to break the dam in your own way. As you do, point out that the breaking of the dam no longer stands for not trusting the Spirit in your lives. Instead, it now illustrates the different responses each of you may have had when receiving Christ and the Spirit. For one, the receiving of the Spirit may have been more gradual, like poking holes in the dam to let the water out. For another receiving the Spirit was more dramatic, like smashing the dam all at once. But regardless of what each of you experienced, make sure your children know their experience is okay whatever it is. Paul, Andrew, and Peter each had his own way of responding, as well.

The following verses referenced in this chapter can be found in sequence on my web site, www.tmoments.com. Click on the Book Resources button located on the home page.

I Peter 3:18; I John 4:13; Acts 9:17-21; Matthew 4:18 –20; Acts 2:2-4; I Corinthians 12: 7, 13; Ephesians 4:4-6; Galatians 5:19-21; Luke 11:39- 42; Galatians 5:22-23; Romans 5:5

CONCLUSION

I hope you have enjoyed doing these 24 Teachable Moments with your children; I believe they can make a difference in their lives as well as yours. As mentioned earlier, I have additional Teachable Moments on my web site from which to draw. Some were written years ago and need revising; I am in the process of doing that right now. Some of the Teachable Moments bare the same name or title as ones in this book, but have varied subject matter and applications. The Teachable Moment in this book about faith leading to salvation, *The Man on the High Flying Trapeze*, is an example. On the web site there are actually four articles on faith called *The Trapeze Series* with a different emphasis and illustration in each one.

Finally, I want to hear about your experience when you complete a Teachable Moment with your children. You can do this by contacting me on my web site (www.tmoments.com), or by emailing me (kent@tmoments.com). And if you have a Teachable Moment you and your children have created, I would love to read it and perhaps even put it on my web site for other parents to enjoy.

God bless, and may your time with your children be an enriching experience as you study and apply the Word together.

Kent McClain

NOTES

Introduction

1. Kent McClain, *Mission Possible* (Sylmar, California: K.M. Publishing Company, 1992), pages 16-17.

Trick or Treat *(Halloween)*

1. Laura Stepp, *Pimpin' For Halloween Goodies* (Washington, D.C.: Washington Post, September 4, 2004). Used with permission.
2. Margaret Galitzin, *What's Good and Evil about Halloween* (Internet: Traditions in Action Incorporated, October 25th, 2007).

The Thanksgiving President *(Thanksgiving)*

1. William J. Johnson, *George Washington the Christian* (New York, Forgotten Books/ Abingdon Press, 1919), pages 28-31.
2. The American College Dictionary, C.L. Barnhart-Chief Editor, *Deism* (New York: Random House, 1963), page 319.
3. William J. Johnson, *George Washington the Christian* (New York, Forgotten Books/ Abingdon Press, 1919), pages 28-31.
4. David Barton, *The Bulletproof George Washington* (Aledo, Texas: Wall Builder Press, 1990), pages 45.
5. David Barton, *The Bulletproof George Washington* (Aledo, Texas: Wall Builder Press, 1990), pages 33-40.
6. David Barton, *The Bulletproof George Washington* (Aledo, Texas: Wall Builder Press, 1990), pages 49-51.
7. William J. Johnson, *George Washington the Christian* (New York, Forgotten Books/ Abingdon Press, 1919), page 173.

Colors and Symbols of Christmas *(Christmas)*

1. Ted Olsen, *The Story of Santa Claus's Namesake/ The Real Saint Nicholas* (Internet: ChrristianHistory.net, Christianity Today, 2008).
2. Susan Seals, *Discovering the Truth about Santa Claus* (Internet: St. Nicholas Center, www.stnicholascenter.org, 2002-2012).
3. Santa Claus, *Saint Nicholas* (Internet: Wikipedia).

The Star of Bethlehem *(Christmas)*

1. Reverend Alfred Edersheim, *The Life and Times of Jesus the Messiah: Volume I* (New York, Longmans, Green, and Company, 1910), pages 211-213.

Lincoln the Christian *(President's Day)*

1. Franklin Graham, *Quote by Abraham Lincoln* (Washington D.C., Inaugural Invocation of President George W. Bush, January 20th, 2001).
2. Jack Keismer, *Bathroom Trivia Book: If At First You Don't Succeed* (Saddle River, New Jersey, Red-Letter Press, Inc., 1986), page 35.
3. William J. Johnson, *Abraham Lincoln the Christian* (Amsterdam, The Netherlands: Fredonia Books, 2004), page 191.
4. Lincoln Memorial Album, O.H. Oldroyd, 1883, page 366 & William J. Johnson, *Abraham Lincoln the Christian* (Amsterdam, The Netherlands: Fredonia Books, 2004), page 172.
5. William J. Johnson, *Abraham Lincoln the Christian* (Amsterdam, The Netherlands: Fredonia Books, 2004), pages 171-172.
6. William J. Johnson, *Abraham Lincoln the Christian* (Amsterdam, The Netherlands: Fredonia Books, 2004), page 182.
7. William J. Johnson, *Abraham Lincoln the Christian* (Amsterdam, The Netherlands: Fredonia Books, 2004), page 107.
8. William J. Johnson, *Abraham Lincoln the Christian* (Amsterdam, The Netherlands: Fredonia Books, 2004), pages 120-121.
9. William J. Johnson, *Abraham Lincoln the Christian* (Amsterdam, The Netherlands: Fredonia Books, 2004), page 176. William J. Johnson, *Abraham Lincoln the Christian* (Amsterdam, The Netherlands: Fredonia Books, 2004), page 172. William J. Johnson, *Abraham Lincoln the Christian* (Amsterdam, The Netherlands: Fredonia Books, 2004), page 182.

The End is Even Better *(Mother's Day)*

1. Irene Temple Bailey, *Parable of Motherhood* (Westwood, New Jersey: Fleming H. Revell Company, 1936), page 9 of Funeral Services by James L. Christensen. Permission to quote was sought from Baker books, the original publisher, and other sources using the story.

Narnia *(Virtuous literature/movies can assist in building your children's faith)*

1. Janet & Geoff Benge, *C.S. Lewis: Master Story Teller* (Seattle, Washington, YWAM Publishing, 2007), pages 85-92.

"No," "Not Yet," "Yes" *(Teaching children what to expect from God when they pray)*

1. Janet & Geoff Benge, *Jacob Deshazer* (Seattle, Washington: YWAM Publishing, 2009), pages 142-154 & back cover of book.
2. Janet & Geoff Benge, *Lillian Trasher* (Seattle, Washington: YWAM Publishing, 2011), pages 186-189 & back cover of book.

Twelve Cans *(Faith)*

1. Janet & Geoff Benge, *Jonathan Goforth* (Seattle, Washington: YWAM publishing, 2001).

God the Father, Son, and Spirit *(Explaining the Trinity to your children)*

1. Wayne Grudem, *Systematic Theology* (Grand Rapids, Michigan: Zondervan, 1994), page 226.

Destinée Media

Destinée Media publishes both fiction and nonfiction and aims to bring a fresh perspective to spirituality and culture.

At Destinée Media we seek to operate by faith in God within a Biblical/Christian worldview. We hope to inspire 'culture-making' by promoting ideas that will contribute to Christ being understood as Lord of the whole of life, which is to be marked by redemption and renewal. We are committed to reflecting carefully on vital matters for the church, academy and society, while aiming to keep a personal and intimate dimension of the Christian life in view.

We thank you for your interest in our materials and hope that you find them both relevant and challenging. Please share your thoughts with us:

www.destineemedia.com

destinēe

www.ingramcontent.com/pod-product-compliance
Lightning Source LLC
Chambersburg PA
CBHW030329080526
44584CB00012B/774